BORN FIRE

Dragon

A MEMOIR

SUSAN KISKIS

Mechanicsburg, Pennsylvania USA

Published by Sunbury Press, Inc.
50 West Main Street, Suite A
Mechanicsburg, Pennsylvania 17055

www.sunburypress.com

Copyright © 2014 by Susan Kiskis.
Cover copyright © 2014 by Sunbury Press, Inc.

Sunbury Press supports copyright. Copyright fuels creativity, encourages diverse voices, promotes free speech, and creates a vibrant culture. Thank you for buying an authorized edition of this book and for complying with copyright laws by not reproducing, scanning, or distributing any part of it in any form without permission. You are supporting writers and allowing Sunbury Press to continue to publish books for every reader. For information contact Sunbury Press, Inc., Subsidiary Rights Dept., 50-A W. Main St., Mechanicsburg, PA 17011 USA or legal@sunburypress.com.

For information about special discounts for bulk purchases, please contact Sunbury Press Orders Dept. at (855) 338-8359 or orders@sunburypress.com.

To request one of our authors for speaking engagements or book signings, please contact Sunbury Press Publicity Dept. at publicity@sunburypress.com.

ISBN: 978-1-62006-505-1 (Trade Paperback)
ISBN: 978-1-62006-506-8 (Mobipocket)
ISBN: 978-1-62006-507-5 (ePub)

FIRST SUNBURY PRESS EDITION: October 2014

Product of the United States of America
0 1 1 2 3 5 8 13 21 34 55

Set in Bookman Old Style
Designed by Lawrence Knorr
Cover by Amber Rendon
Edited by Amanda Shrawder

Continue the Enlightenment!

"We're all just walking each other home."
                              Baba Ram Dass

CHAPTER 1

It's Nathan Lane. He's looking at me. I mean I know it's really not Nathan Lane, but my brain can't interpret infinite power and knowledge, so it's giving me Nathan Lane.

I'm in a dream of sorts and here is the Tony award-winning actor from *The Bird Cage,* and Carrie's good friend from *Sex in the City* who was gay, but decided to marry a straight woman. Nathan Lane, dressed up in a white suit that shimmers in the light surrounding him, is what my brain has decided God looks like. He stands there patiently waiting for me, flashing that bright Broadway smile. Where are we? Standing on clouds that don't really look all together like puffs of condensed air and water? Instead, I realize we are in the place between heaven and earth—the place where sometimes, during deep meditations, I meet those from the other side. It's like a popular coffee house where there is no limit to slices of zen and good company. He's waiting for me.

Nathan Lane (aka God) asks, "So, do you want to stay or do you want to go?"

I knew this moment was coming for about a year now. I could feel it in my bones. I had hoped to be awake for this moment, to make a conscious choice, but here I was, my soul standing before him while my body was nestled under an abundance of covers and pushed up against my husband Charlie.

"I need time to think," I said. *Stupid. Stupid.* This is what happens when you allow your soul to do the talking. Time. Time for what?

I used to be painfully afraid of death. Even though I had these experiences that all added up to me knowing there was more aside from this so-called-life on Earth, I had no need to go. Been there, done that, many times I was sure. However, in the past year I started to make peace with the concept of death. I allowed it to creep up on

1

me like a good story, wiggle its way into my mind and settle comfortably there. Now I was deciding whether I was fine with death, right here in this moment. Was I ready to go? I read somewhere once, perhaps in a Sylvia Brown book, that we have a certain number of "outs" in our lives. "Outs" are choices as to whether we wanted to stay or go. I guess here was another "out" option for me. I didn't want to take this option. I want to grow old well into my nineties and squeeze the nectar out of life. Left up to my soul now, would I make the same decision my mind would make?

I know death well. I've seen its face three times in my personal life and many times with others. Death and I, we're old buddies.

BOOK 1

CHAPTER 2

Fire Dragon

I was born in the year of the dragon in 1976. Not just the year of the dragon, the year of the red fire dragon, the most passionate and violent of all of the dragons. In Chinese Astrology, each lunar year begins a new cycle of twelve animals, each of which are associated with an element. I could have been an Earth Dragon, a Water Dragon, a Metal Dragon, or a Wood Dragon. I however, am a fire dragon.

I came into this world later than my due date with the most perfectly formed solid head, I am told. My parents said my doctor called me the most beautiful baby he ever delivered. I am sure Obstetrician's say that to every mother and father.

In New York City's Lennox Hill Hospital, I met my father, a World War II Veteran, James Alexander, who was in his late forties, a skinny man with thin white hair and on his second marriage. My mother who pushed me out into the world (while high on the drugs given to women in labor at the time) was a twenty-something-year-old Yugoslavian immigrant on her second marriage, as well. A short woman with a thick accent and a love for the U.S., she and my father had only been together for a little more than a year before I arrived. I already had seven half-brothers and sisters between the two of my parents.

My father grew up in an on and off again impoverished family during the Great Depression where at one point his father, James Aloysius, had to take a job as a janitor. My grandmother, Gladys was from Wales and raised my father and his brother John. Much of what I know about my father came from files I discovered after he passed on or my mother's exaggerated tales. My mother's tales included how his family was related to the Kennedys. Files in a briefcase told me he was a Military Police Officer stationed in Italy during World War II. My father's only story about his life was how, when he was a little boy, he portrayed a detective in a school play and got to chew gum for the part.

My mother, however, for all of her embellishments, was easier to learn about. My maternal family was from Montenegro, yet considered themselves Albanian due to heritage. I was always puzzled why they ignored the Sicilian immigrant part of our bloodline, even when it seemed so many of them immigrated through Italy before living in the U.S. I myself spent many years of my adult life attempting to learn Italian. All I can remember is *Chiami la polizia, La Dolce Vita,* and *uno grappolo.* Of course there are words like *prego, grazie, per favore,* simple everyday words and phrases I know. I wanted to hear the words of Italy, my heritage, spill from my lips, pouring off my tongue like I am expelling a bad habit.

Growing up on a farm, herding sheep, and sleeping on the floor with all of her family in one room, was not something my mother was fond of. With six brothers and sisters of her own, and being the middle child, she couldn't wait to escape.

As a child, my mother who had little education—being in a third world country, and being a girl—once told my grandmother Katrina something shocking:

"One day, I am going to move to the United States!"

My grandmother asked, "How do you even know such a word? We never told you that."

For a woman of the customary Albanian traditions, and little more than an elementary school education, this was not something that would be feasible—nor was it explicable how she heard of this country.

When my mother was sixteen she was married off to an Albanian thirteen years her senior who brought her to live in Italy. All the women in my family had arranged marriages. Usually business was conducted through the male seeing the girl at a wedding, a family gathering, or sometimes from family pushing a photo of their soon-to-be eligible daughter in front of a single man. The woman saw her husband the day she got married. From there came a whole host of customary wedding traditions, which included the bride looking through her wedding ring, peaking in from a doorway and saying, "Oy," for each guest at the wedding she could see—that and pretty much looking depressed during the wedding and reception while the husband had a grand time.

From Italy, my mother and her husband moved to the U.S. where she gave birth to my sister, Mary. In her early twenties, my mother's husband asked her to leave. He said to her, "You are not pretty enough. You gave me a girl and I wanted a son. I made a decision that even though I married you in a church, I want to get married six times." My mom was unfortunately wife number four.

With no knowledge of the English language, she stayed with family, learned English, got a job, went to school in Boston, moved back to NYC, became a private investigator and got a gun permit. She made it on local news for being the first woman who was not a government employee and was a private investigator with a gun permit. My sister was raised by her father, as was our culture's custom.

My father, meanwhile, had married young, lived in Connecticut with six children and his Yugoslavian wife, and had prestigious jobs working at Paramount Pictures and MacMillan Publishing. That is, until his uncontrollable thirst for alcohol—and subsequent physical abuse—took over his life, leaving him with nothing. When he met my mother, he had to borrow money from her to take her out to dinner.

When I was born, my father was so elated to be given a second chance to have a family again. My mother felt the same way, even though she was not in love with him. She focused on creating a home. Growing up impoverished motivated my mother to want the best of the best. Finances were not a concern for her, just things like a new sofa, pretty petite coffee cups, golden lamps for end tables. My father spread his money around—to my mother, a bar, and to anywhere he could gamble, like the local OTB (off-track betting where one could bet on horses).

I saw my sister, Mary, on and off while I was a child. My father's children however, were scarce. In their teens, only two of them, Liam and Connor, would visit us. I have no memory, only photos.

As my memory grew and my mother's belly swelled with my brother, my father's old habits kicked back into action. Drinking, blacking out and hitting my mother (and not knowing why she was so upset with him the next day, with welts and bruised skin) became the norm in our household. My brother and I had issues getting along since I could remember. My mother thought perhaps it was because I was jealous of the attention—him getting a bottle and a pacifier—but as we got older nothing changed. We moved to Fort Lauderdale, Florida when I was around five. My father was born in Melbourne and his brother now lived in Florida. I loved my Uncle John, who on one occasion gave me the largest teddy bear, which was unfortunately destroyed a few years later by my brother in a wrestling match.

During those times my brother, a little tot, begged me to play with him daily. My mother started to beg me too. I remember clearly one day doing everyone a favor, taking the high road and playing with him. We lived in a motel at the time due to the scarcity of money. We ran around the bed over and over again laughing like children should. We did this until he fell and hit his head on the corner of the steel bed frame leading to an ER visit, which provided him with an ample amount of stitches. I actually felt horrible for him. I cared. However, my mother blamed me of injuring him on purpose, which put an end to me wanting to play with him again. From then on, it was a rarity, but I made exceptions—such as putting makeup on him and doing his hair in trade for playtime. Or, the G.I. Joes would have to be incorporated with Barbie dolls and My Little Ponies, but it had to be nice. I didn't like the battles he liked to engage over plastic mountains.

My father—who seemed never really present in our lives—provided me with such a love for him, but disdain for his age. The heart longs for what is absent it seems. A child at the motel asked if he was my grandfather to which I said angrily, "He is my father!" That scar went so deep into my psyche that as I grew up, I swore I'd never have children after the age of thirty—it was just morally wrong.

The few instances my father did spend time with me was when trying to teach me how to swim. Unknowingly damaging me with a deep fear of water, he would dunk me when he said he wouldn't and let go of me in the water, trying to get me to sink or swim (and hoping it would be the swimming). I declared at five after one final lie from him, I would never get in the water with him again. My mother tried getting me swimming lessons, but they failed, as I was too afraid to let go of the edge of the pool. My father made it up with fireworks displayed around the holidays—which wooed my mom with shiny colors, but made her think we were all going to catch on fire.

I knew our family was different from others even at that young age. I couldn't put my finger on it, but we were. It was the way people looked at me, or didn't talk to me. I went to Pre-Kindergarten where a group of kids I wanted to be friends with, didn't want to be friends with me. So, I played alone with my one Barbie that was naked half the time (I had no idea what I did with her clothes). My mother said I would go check on my brother—in the other end of the building at the attached daycare—and change him, as he was always wet and the caretakers there didn't clean him up, while she was at work.

We moved back to New York City after living in Florida for only a short time. My mother enrolled me in first grade. Due to our financial constraints, we lived in a hotel. I had skipped kindergarten altogether because of a score on a test, but first grade was already part way through their year before I started. I had to work extra hard to catch up to all of the other children.

While my mother helped me with homework as much as she could, she couldn't write English better than a young child, and she only knew basic math. I remember staying up late into the evening doing homework and going to bed with a meager meal of bread and milk in a bowl. Big fights happened often in that little room. I could not tell you about what happened or what was being said, but only the large emotion that colored the room—like reds and golds being flicked here and there.

After school, I attended The Girls and Boys Club, which nurtured and opened me up into a different world. New

York being New York, my caretakers and friends were multifaceted, multicolored and full of love in their own ways. I tasted radishes, went to movies, went to museums, and learned songs like *Ebony and Ivory*. But even there, my life would catch up with me.

My mother grew up in an all white culture and my father during segregation. When my father was drunk, he turned into a horrible racist. I remember befriending a little black boy to whom I was instructed never to speak with again. I recall walking down the street with my father as he slung hateful words at a black man for no good reason. For these many reasons, instead of hate, they grew seeds of tolerance, a rebellious nature against my social norm, and a love for everyone regardless of who they were. That little boy was just like me. Little, wanted to play, and was a friend. There was no difference in my eyes.

I would hear the conversations with multiple after-school providers, telling my mother they couldn't keep staying late for her to pick me up. A teacher told me they would buy me a butterfly sticker for my book on a field trip, but could not keep buying me things—I needed to bring my own money. I remember taking my plastic blue and green iridescent bubble butterfly sticker and placing it in a book of mine like it was the most treasured thing in the world. I had no money for anything. My mother had nothing to give me at the time. I was deeply ashamed and embarrassed. I never asked for anything again from my afternoon caretakers at the Boys and Girls Club.

I was chronically sick as a child with inner ear infections. One time at the Boys and Girls Club I ran a really high fever. They brought me into a room, laid blanket after blanket on top of me, and when my mother arrived, I was taken home to an ice bath. Ice baths as a child were the bane of my existence.

Often my mother would take me to the ER when my temperature would get extremely high where as she would tell me in my later years, they would put ice blankets on me. My trips to the ER were frequent since my mother was instilled with panic when an ear infection and fever turned into a coma when I was two.

The doctors told her I would never fully recover, if I woke up. A woman, Maria, who babysat me quite often, told my mother one evening to go home and rest. She would sit with me.

Maria was very faithful to her Catholic religion, possibly more so than my mother was. One night, Maria sat with me and prayed all night. The next morning, I am told, she said to my mother, "Suzie will wake up in a few hours." To everyone's surprise, that's exactly what I did. However, the questions then came as to how I went into a coma in the first place and ideas were tossed around that someone gave me the "evil eye," a theory I remember being brought up with until my pre-teen years.

Maria, who would secretly teach me Spanish words upon my begging, as my father did not want me to learn any languages other than English. He didn't want me growing up with an accent, which was such an odd choice since he married two foreign women and his own mother was an immigrant. Perhaps he saw the discrimination of immigrants?

Maria was matter-of-fact with child rearing, but always cleaned me, fed me, and would not bark about lack of payment from my mother in front of me. Having never had children, and with an alcoholic husband of her own, Maria knew much about how to care for a child. And while her husband, Danny, was not violent like my father, she suffered as my mother did with paying bills. I loved Maria and Danny so much. Danny was softer than Maria, being a joker and giving me what I wanted, while Maria was more practical about what a child needed—like I didn't need another Barbie doll. She instead made clothes for me, her prime income being a seamstress.

My other sitter, who I called my Nana, was from Croatia and used to babysit my brother and me along with her grandson, Matty. Nana was straight forward with how to care for a child. My brother and I were fed, bathed, taken for exercise, forced to nap, and had organized playtime. Nana loved her soap operas, like my mother, so naptime seemed to fall into those time slots if we were with her on a weekday. Nana was family to me and I clung to her, looking to fill some imaginary hole in my heart. However, she was unable or unwilling to provide that for me. So, at the end of the day, I was once again a source of money issues with my Nana asking my mother for payment and my mother asking for more time.

My years of moving around from one place to another finally settled when I was around seven years old. My parents rented the top floor apartment in a building in Astoria, NY owned by a Greek woman who lived a floor below us. Angela became a grandmother to me. I learned to cook while she talked to me in broken English, and occasionally Greek, and supplied me with an endless amount of hugs. Angela tried to get me to teach her how to write English and she would teach me Greek, but at a young age, I did not have the patience to stick to it, getting frustrated with teaching her at every turn.

In school I excelled and started feeling a bit more normal as our household and finances stabilized. My sister, Mary, started visiting at least once a week. My brother and I still had a rough time interacting with one another as I did not like him and he was now worse having gotten into wrestling. My sister however, we could talk about girl stuff. She was older, wiser, and when at our house, she could forgo the mandatory long skirt and shirt uniform of her father's Albanian household for a pair of jeans, t-shirt and leather jacket.

While we mostly interacted with my mother's Albanian family outside of the walls of our home, when they came, the house got fully involved in preparing. We had to get buckets of feta cheese (which was easy living in a Greek community), scallions, peppers, slices of meat and then douse them with salt. The cabinets became full of Turkish coffee and grappa (a very strong eastern European alcohol). My brother and I were to be quiet children who did not play loudly; we were to be present for long lengths of time, to be doted on in Albanian, and go through the triple kiss welcome to women and men wearing dark layers of clothes. We were never short a Ya-Ya in the group.

When we had to leave to visit family (and there was always family to visit—hundreds of cousins), the events would be a marathon. It was impolite to interrupt my mother to find out where the bathroom was and if I was tired, too bad. Sometimes I fell asleep near the coats on someone's bed or dozed off on the sofas if at the end of the day there finally was a spot for a child to sit on.

The strongest memory is that of the smell. Albanians all smelled the same to me—sweaty. They did not seem to partake in deodorant. I could not stand to be in the same room with two people, let alone fifty; the longer we were there, the worse it got and the triple kiss goodbyes from a child's height were the worst.

However, even though the days were long, boring and smelly, it was there I had some of my most important influences—listening to a language I could not speak or write, but through emphasis and exposure, could manage to follow along. Growing up in NYC with so many unique cultures—and being entrenched in one of them—gave me the gift of understanding accents. It was also a culture entrenched in mystery and prayer. Things like the "evil eye" (someone eying you up and praying for something bad to happen to you), dreams and what they meant, coffee readings where after one's Turkish, black molasses-looking coffee would be drunk, the cup would be flipped over to dry, revealing messages from the other side. *Your daughter will marry in the next six months. Your money will be compromised soon due to an unforeseen expense. You have death at your door.*

It was here in these places, and in the house of my best friend Sonia, whose mother was from Croatia, where my exposure to the magic of the world began.

My small experiences, which I mention later in my story, were not always accepted by my mother and her family. If I had a gut instinct or a dream, that would be worthy of reflection. A child walking around frustrated she could not paint like she used to in a past life—that was beyond their scope of belief and fell into the *Oh Suzie. You have such an active imagination.*

I specifically remember seeing myself sitting at a canvas in a dream painting a landscape. Aggravation followed me well into my twenties with my current inability to paint, but knowing I had this inherent skill hidden through oceans of time. My hand would not work the brush as it should. My strokes were off, too thick and my ability to paint things I saw in detail would not transfer to canvas. As a child I was not exposed to past lives, but there was an inner knowing, for lack of a better explanation, until I started to catch up to what was "real" and shelved those thoughts.

In my elementary school days we had to do a project about a country. I immediately knew it had to be on Egypt. But how to get magazine pictures about Egypt for my collage? I refused to compromise. I felt so attached to this country, with little understanding why.

A neighbor on the first floor was an Egyptian who read palms. He did not do it professionally, but in a conversation, he let it slip. My mother, who was so desperate for something to happen in her life to get her away from her abusive husband, would seek him out as a second opinion when Sonia's mother was not available or when she wanted to see if someone got another message for her.

Usually I would be kept away from this and told to babysit my brother in our home. One time I asked the Egyptian to read my palm. He looked at it, made a strange face which was a cross between interested and painful, folded my palm and waved me away with some comment about how he could not read my palm because I was a child. I was to stop the silliness and go play. But, I wanted to know about my life, too. Like how many more times was I going to have to play with my brother in the apartment's garage while the cops came over my house to interrupt the "domestic situation?"

My brother and I attended a Catholic school across the street from my home, which further nurtured the link to another world. I became engrossed in prayer, acts of contrition and connecting with God. After learning how to do the "Hail Mary" prayer in sign language, I became mesmerized by this woman. I read stories of saints. I attended the church next door to my school every Sunday with my mother and brother, which was now far more interesting to me than in my younger childhood years when I would be constantly awoken by my mother as I slipped into sleep in the pew at St. Patrick's Cathedral.

Most Precious Blood looked like a medieval stone fort on the outside. When you crossed the threshold, the space opened wide, hugging you with light streaming in from stained glass windows that I think were the stations of the cross. Rows upon rows of pews led their way to a set of steps guarding a large altar where Jesus hung on a cross, visible to all. I now had to sit towards the front of the church, which irked my mother, because I read somewhere that when you sat in the back, the devil had an easier time getting you.

CHAPTER 3

Death Comes Slowly

My mother always let life happen to her. She was not one to seek and find. She was more comfortable in the flow of life. She would react and flow. However, this did not stop her from having deep seeded phobias, which went way past the superstitions of her family.

During thunderstorms, my mother would wake my brother and I taking us into the bathroom. We would wait out the storm so we did not get struck by lightning. One time, after whining for the hundredth time about how tired I was, she said one of her cousins got struck by lightning while sitting right by her front door.

When the occasional minor earthquake or hurricane came into action, we went into the apartment's basement until it was safe. During an impending hurricane, I became so concerned that I gathered all of my stuffed animals and precious toys piling them on top of my bed and covered them with a large sheet to protect them. Needless to say, I was irritated to have to put them all away when the coast was clear.

I became so panicked by life itself that I could not step on a crack, could not step under a ladder, and having to babysit my brother as we got older would throw me into panic attacks. I slowly became afraid of crossing the street and being run over by a car. I remember sitting in the backseat of a car going over a bridge in NYC and having a quiet panic attack about falling off the bridge. However, the one thing my mother told my brother and me endlessly that I never fully bought into was, "Don't laugh or something bad will happen to you." Whenever my brother and I would play and would be laughing or watching something on television that was a hoot, out came my mother reminding us, "Don't laugh or something bad will happen to you."

My brother, who had asthma, was coddled as a child, while I was told to buck up and do what I was told. When my panic attacks ensued, breathing became impossible and felt like a knife was being plunged into my lungs. At the time, no one knew what I was suffering from. I was told to breathe it out or sit down. I also started having TMJ along with issues with my vision. When my body was finally greeted with my monthly visitor, my vision would turn to black, my hearing would dissolve into a high-pitched ring, and I started to feel faint.

I loved watching television. We had the limited television channels everyone had in the eighties and like children of that time, looked forward to Saturday morning and after school cartoons, when we could watch them. However, my mother, like many other mothers in the area, would kick us out to go play with our friends. On the sidewalks we would learn to skateboard, play tag, and invent games. Inside, however, my father started buying me Shirley Temple videos after VHS players came out. I loved watching her. I started mimicking commercial ads and actors. My mother saw that potential and found an agent for my brother and me. Her kids were going to be famous! This became another one of my mother's mantras, which was a good break from being told something was going to kill us—like lightening or a man on the street.

The pattern of our days started changing; instead of being with friends after school, we were shuttled on subway after subway, walking block after block, to audition for modeling gigs, television shows, educational videos and commercials. After a few short years and hundreds of auditions, my brother and I got work, but not without telling my mother how much I hated every minute of having to go to auditions.

Along with that change came my mother's absence in the evenings. As our life stabilized, she got more work as a private investigator with the majority of her work being in the evenings. Most of her clients were restaurants and she had to go sit and have dinner and drinks at the bar to see who was stealing. At home, on the occasional evening my mother did not bring us take out, I became responsible for cooking dinner for my father and brother; though, with little cooking education because my mother could only cook four things—chicken, steak, cabbage, and potatoes.

My father was happy with this arrangement, as girls were to learn to cook, sew, iron, carry a purse and wear a dress. So, he made sure to give me his handkerchiefs to iron and socks to sew during these times, while my brother got to play. At the time I didn't despise these requests from my father. He was hardly home and I wanted nothing more in the world than to please him and make him proud of me. The few times he did spend time with me were mostly spent taking me to a bar with him, where I had my Shirley Temple, or to the OTB. One time he came through on his promise to hang out with my brother and me and took us to Coney Island. I remember it was the first and only time he promised to do something with us and did. I don't remember how we got there or got home. I remember walking with my father and seeing a large ship at a dock. To a child's eyes the ship was like a gigantic creature in the water, wooden glossy boards making its skin, poles up to the skyline. We had hot dogs. I remember thinking how Coney Island didn't look so clean. This day though, even with little memory, has caked in it a promise made good, a day with my father.

My mother had one set of rules and chores for me while my brother had no rules and no chores, which became a constant topic of argument. Between my father's old-fashioned mind and my mother's old-fashioned culture, I was the girl and with that came expectations. My brother, a boy, had little to do except be pleasant and funny, which he did well.

As I grew up, my mother's mantras for me changed once again. The first one was, "You are going to have to be responsible and take care of your brother, your father and myself." And for this she meant at that time in small ways and as an adult for always. I became a master of managing my time between homework, household chores, playing with friends, and prayer. I had to be successful. I set a timeline for myself. I must become a famous singer by the time I was sixteen. An acting career would do, but singing and song writing was my passion. By this time, I was a master of singing in the shower, in my room, all around the house, and in the church choir. I could belt out *Holy Night* louder than anyone, not realizing I should not. When my voice wouldn't go where it should, I mouthed the sounds. For Christmas Eve, I poorly played my electronic keyboard and sang carols for my mother. I included my brother in this skit, but his patience for a long performance did not seem to not match my enthusiasm.

Her second mantra was, "Don't ever trust a man." As I grew up, my mother would add this onto any story of any boy I liked, any experience with a man she'd had, or even in relation to television shows.

We played musical bedrooms at home halfway through my time in Astoria: my father got my brother's bedroom, my brother got mine, and I had to share with my mother. We had the largest room in our apartment with a queen sized bed and huge TV. We even had our own half bath with lilac tiles lining the walls.

I hated not having my own room to talk on the phone with my friends in privacy, and I had to share her esthetic taste of bright colors and shiny objects, which was vastly different from my own reserved black and white or earth tone nature. She hated the color black, for it meant death. I loved the color black and preferred black clothes over anything else.

We also conflicted in our schedules. I was an early bird. She liked to sleep in and wasn't functional until she had consumed two cups of coffee. I needed to go to sleep early, but she needed to watch the eleven o'clock news and every Wednesday evening, I believe it was, *Dallas*. J.R. was one of the perfect examples of why I couldn't trust a man.

My sister, Mary, had an arranged marriage her father created. Breaking with tradition, my mother had secretly devised opportunities for them to meet at our apartment so they could learn about one another. Her husband was sweet, quiet, and spoke limited English. I didn't like him because to me he was old and she was just turning eighteen. He may have only been in his twenties at the time, but when you are a pre-teen, anyone who's not, is old.

Common with our Albanian culture, my sister had two weddings. One was with her family and the second, that my mother, brother and I attended, was with Mary's new husband's family. We danced in circles (much like an Irish baptism party I once attended), ate lots of food, and did customary practices, like walking by the banquet table shaking the hands of the groom, my brother-in-law. We grabbed pepper from the table tossed some onto the bathroom floor, pressing our shoes deliberately into the grinds to avoid slippery shoes. My sister stayed standing for most of the reception at the banquet table looking down with no smile, as was our tradition. I saw Mary on and off for about a year after she married. Then suddenly, she stopped talking with us. I had no idea why Mary would abandon our relationship. I was told she didn't want to have anything to do with us anymore.

The last day of, possibly sixth grade, before Thanksgiving break, I came home to piles of groceries in brown paper bags left on the steps near our apartment door. I was the first one to come home and encounter these bags. I read the note that came with it, and dropped to the floor embarrassed and crying. The note indicated the food was from my school saying they helped families in need during the holidays. When my mother arrived home, I demanded she throw it in the trash or give it back to the school telling them they were wrong. My mother was having a difficult time paying our tuition and the school was naturally being kind. Growing up, my mother said I was never allowed to tell anyone what was going on in our home, so I had this natural shame. It was one thing to get into an argument with my mother about me sharing my parents' strife with my best friend, but it was another subject when people knew we were poor. That Thanksgiving, however, we ate what the church gave us.

A year later, my father came home drunk, which was no exception to most days in my life. And he beat my mother, which was not unusual. He swore. He yelled in a drunken rage. He knocked her unconscious with our white painted wooden bedroom door.

The house suddenly grew silent. Only for a moment.

"Fila, get up," my father drunkenly shouted. He repeated again, "Fila, get up." This time he laughed.

I walked over towards her body lying on the carpeted floor. She did not move. I knelt down to see if she was alive. She looked dead. I grew numb, feeling like she was fine, maybe even faking it to not have to get up and take more. Rage swelled inside me. The dead didn't move and neither did she. "You killed mom!" I shouted.

"She's not dead. She's faking it," my father said. It gave my mind the reassurance it needed that my mother was alive. My gut was not taken seriously. I needed rational, concrete knowledge.

He continued to chuckle to himself, swaying from side to side, unable to hold his balance. My mother started to slowly awaken, eyes looking around in confusion, whispering my brother and my name.

My anger for my father boiled up in my chest. To me, my mother was always the weak one. My father was the strong one. Today though, he was weak. I saw it in his eyes. Glassy, bloodshot eyes like that of a young calf. They looked like no one was there. I grabbed my lip gloss and with glittery pink liquid in hand, painted the letter x on his chest. I had no idea what led me to do this, but it was the only way at the moment I could express my rage.

I don't remember who called the police. Most likely it was me. My brother and I were told to go downstairs by the police. My brother and I played in our apartment's plain cement garage, which was filled with random boxes, yard tools, and such. We rode around in small circles while the police and emergency care were upstairs with my mother and father. I remember lying, even though I refused to do so anymore. A young officer with short sun-kissed blond hair and a stiff walk asked us if we were OK. Defensive at heart, I quickly replied nonchalantly, "We always play in here," which was my way of saying, *It's none of your business buddy, keep on walking.*

In my later years, I would laugh upon discovering how my name is derived from Hebrew and means honesty and trust. As a young child, I came to a point where I could not lie anymore. It made me sick to my stomach. When bill collectors would call for my mother, I one day refused to lie to them anymore. I could no longer say she wasn't home. I would answer the phone and hold the phone in her direction. My inability to protect her would bring her to tears. As a young child, I could not understand the pain of dealing with financial issues. I could only start to learn self-preservation of my own. Here I was breaking that promise to myself to conceal my embarrassment.

My mother did not let my father come back home after this time. She sold all of her jewelry at the local pawnshops. I remember we went with her for days on end to a variety of places, most of them located on Broadway in Astoria. She sold all of her favorite pieces to care for us. For a meager amount, she turned over her beloved gold and onyx choker and diamond tennis bracelet, along with many more pieces she collected over the years.

One time, shortly after the incident, walking back from the movies, I thought I saw a man that looked like my father sleeping on a bench on the street. I told my mother, and she responded, "I heard that he might be homeless." I never asked again. In my mind, though, I secretly felt ashamed for him and wanted to rescue him.

Within a few months, my mother started talking incessantly to a man, Matt, who worked in radio, first as a disc jockey, and then sales, and then management. He was over six feet all, medium build with olive skin and dark hair, vastly different from my skinny father with white, thinning hair. He grew up in the south where he met many famous people including Elvis Presley.

While I could not see what my mother saw in him, she called him, in her accent, "saxy." They met in a bar in Manhattan where he wooed my mother with tales of his airplane and money, when in reality he was just as broke as she was. He lived in Virginia Beach at the time and my mother spent countless hours on the phone giggling like a teenage girl.

At the time I did not think of my mother's happiness as anything special, just annoying that she would ignore my brother and I, like she did when we took our summer vacations in Atlantic City. On these trips, she spent all of her time in the casino and when my brother and I ran out of money or things to do, we would need to sit on the carpet a few feet away from the entrance of the casino, waiting for her return. The casino guards made sure to always watch that we never stepped over the lines separating the two spaces, marked by different carpets meeting in one singular place.

When visiting Virginia Beach, we spent most of our time at the beach so my mother could sun bathe. My brother and I made friends, got seriously burned, and enjoyed the sidewalk. As a non-swimmer, I learned to boogie board and jump waves, one time almost drowning.

Death is a very unique experience. It happens in slow motion. As much as I tried to stretch my arms above to the surface, the waves pummeled me down. Up I went for a breath, mouth opened wide to the sun, and slam! Another wave pushed me down. And another one. And another one. My body rippled through the violent conflict of water below the surface. I could not stop the seawater from entering my lungs. My feet would touch the ground and then fly up bringing me into a horizontal position before the water stuffed me back down towards the millions of bits of sand, shells and rocks. Murky green water was all around me, inside of me. I couldn't fight anymore. I started to accept the inevitable fact that I was going to die. It was only then, as my eyes shut, a hand grabbed me and dragged me to shore.

On the sand, I was slapped hard and told to cough out the salt water. I lay caked in sand now, surrounded by jellyfish, and some angry adults wondering why I went so deep into the ocean. There was no time for me to mourn for my almost fatality. I needed to buck up and move on with my day.

Matt had a modest book collection. I lost myself in his books on astrology. I would apply thick coats of aloe to my charred skin and lay on the sofa soaking in the different signs. I then moved on to dream books and back to more astrology books.

I learned astrology, in its simplest terms, was based on when you were born. I was born December 6th so I was a Sagittarius. It was where the sun was in the sky the day I was born. When you read your horoscope, you and everyone around the approximate thirty day timeline would have your future told to you based on where the sun currently was in the sky and what planets it interacted with, including the moon. On a deeper level, which I did not know at the time, you could find out your natal chart, which is where everything was in the sky when you were born. It is so rare that it's like a fingerprint. It can only represent you and any other person born at that exact minute at your exact location.

My mother married Matt within a year of our first visit to Virginia. My mother wore pink to the wedding. Mother's best friend, Tia, and Mike's father and stepmother, accompanied my brother and I. My mother didn't tell her family she was remarrying because that was so taboo they might never speak with her again. That was to be another secret I was never to share. This one was easier, as I rarely saw and spoke to my mother's family as I grew older.

A few weeks after the wedding, we moved to Winston Salem, North Carolina, where Matt had gotten a new job. We packed moved from our apartment, packed up all of our belongings and made our way to a new life. My mother, who was used to public transit and could not drive, became bored quickly. She had nothing to do in this place while her husband worked. When he came home, he was tired and wanted to talk about work, have dinner, and go to sleep.

We visited the school I would attend the following September. The children all looked like aliens to me in their plain-Jane appearance with no makeup and polos, t-shirts and jeans. They seemed to mirror the same expression back to me as I stood there with my teased bangs, makeup, and tutu skirt hovering over matching leggings. I dreaded going to this school.

In NC, I experienced our first tornado which ripped trees from roots and seemed to hit every other house. While our home remained unscathed, we lived without water and electricity for about a week. Food, like the town, got boring real quick.

Matt lost his job almost as soon as he got it. We moved back to New York. In Astoria, we lived in a studio apartment where my brother and I were constantly told to leave to play with friends or visit our next door neighbor, my Nana, who kept complaining to my mother she couldn't always watch us. My mother became pregnant with twins and was delighted, while Matt couldn't stand living in one room or New York. From the south, he needed fresh air and open land. My mother, however, was in her happy place living once again in NY where she could access any place at any time. Not much time passed before my mother miscarried. She was devastated as she had names picked out and a dream of an expanded family. Matt looked for ways out of New York and was successful in finding a job in Towson, Maryland, where he rented a condo in a walkable area for my mother. Halfway through my eighth grade of school, we moved again.

Matt started his a job as a General Manager for a local talk radio station. I started school in another country for all I knew. I hailed from the land of Madonna-like fashions, teased hair (although it was much lower by the time I was in eighth grade), ripped jeans, and short shorts (which were a great alternative to triangle shorts). I entered a version of the Stepford wives. Most girls had long blond hair pulled back in ponytails with t-shirts, soccer shorts, and white Keds, which they wrote all over. While we lived in the Penthouse of a condominium building, everyone was a good homeowner with the most perfectly mowed grass treated by Chemlawn. There were few people who weren't jocks or wanted to be jocks. I had never heard of the popular sports, lacrosse, or field hockey. I had never picked up a tennis racket. I had never run a mile before.

One month after we moved to Towson, I had a dream of me walking on a street with a boy from school. The devil appeared and in my dreams I started praying the Hail Mary over and over again. I was surrounded by light and started to levitate in a protective white bubble before I woke up. Months later, as I started to familiarize myself with my new landscape, I found the street from my dream.

These types of intuitive nightmares during my teenage years never ceased. I kept learning how to use prayer in dreams to escape evil. I also learned how to control my nightmares. Instead of running in slow motion, like I was stuck in molasses, or called out for help in a whisper, I stopped my dream in place, like pressing pause on a remote control, recognize and resolve the problem, or just tell myself I was dreaming, and woke up. As someone who primarily only had nightmares and rarely dreams, this tool was invaluable.

Let me for a moment introduce you to the rock star of all angels—Michael. When I was twelve, he introduced himself to me like a person would; only, there was nothing to touch because he was not incarnate. Michael has a uniform of a robe that can be white or black when he is in work mode. In a casual mood, he likes to sport jeans and a leather jacket. His long dark-blond locks wave down towards his shoulders and he has a scar across his right cheek. One minute he can be the strongest warrior and the next asking if he looks good. That Michael—so vain!

The only way to describe the next few years was to say that Michael was training me. What was he training me for? Who knows, but I could only say that at the time I believed he was training me to a) be a warrior of evil, and b) teaching me how to block out negativity from my life and energy field.

I had no basis on how to comprehend what was happening in my world for no one I knew at the time was into holistic experiences. My mother had her religious and mysterious culture where she could appreciate that I prayed to Mary and she would protect me from evil. She could accept an angel was protecting me. My step-father had his toe dipped into astrology, but no one could explain how I knew what I knew. There was no separation from my religious points of view and these odd encounters. During my senior year of high school, I would even wake up some mornings really early and head to church a few blocks from my home. I did not need anyone to go with me. Even if I just needed to pop over for a quick prayer or confession, I went with no second thought.

Acclimating to a new environment with an altogether different sense of fashion, priorities and lifestyle, was difficult at best. It took time to assimilate to the culture around me and find kindred spirits. My mother kept my brother and I occupied by spoiling us with the newest technology, shopping and food. She was a stay-at-home mom now who loved her husband very much, but could not stand cocktail hour on the balcony with my stepfather because all he did was talk about work.

Like women depicted on Anne Taintor napkins, she slowly became more and more depressed being at home in a small downtown with few friends and nothing to do. My mother was never the domestic kind. Soon she started seeing a psychiatrist in the building where we lived and partook of Prozac, which led to extreme highs and lows and made her a spending machine. QVC made lots of money during those years.

I enjoyed being a good kid, but also getting into mild trouble. I started smoking, and my best friend and I used to sneak out with boys when we were supposed to be at the movies. I met Tommy when I was a sophomore. An adopted, attractive boy who presented me with a dozen long stemmed red roses, never tried to make a move on me, only incessantly romance me. Growing into myself, I naturally turned away from his affections, starting to choose the pursuit rather than the easy fruit. This was not a pattern I would stray from. Out of the few boyfriends I had in high school—the incredibly sweet skinny Dom, who despite his frame could pin me down in a second when we wrestled, to a boy I dated from a private school—all of these dear men were out of luck. I sought the long-haired senior musician or the boy I sat next to in Science class that made fun of me.

While I started to enjoy the benefits of hard liquor, my stepfather had stopped drinking and started going to AA meetings. He also became a born again Christian. All of my dearly beloved astrology books were thrown out. He called them works from the devil. I could no longer wear perfume around him as its scent reminded him of alcohol. He withdrew into solitude as my mother racked up the bills shopping from her bed in her pajamas all day long. All I could do to get her attention every now and then was to pick dandelions on the way home for her. Poetry I that I wrote, dedicated to her, was lost on her.

While Matt held no affection for me and I could cope with that, my brother who longed for a father suffered. Matt asked to adopt my brother and I when he and my

mother first married. My brother and I simply stated we
already had a father. We did not know how deep that cut
must have run, even though we could not at a young age
understand what we said was hurtful.

My brother did not get the father he sought; rather, he
stayed away from us when possible. We never did right. I
got yelled at if I changed the thermostat in the house. I got
yelled at for singing too much or too loudly. My brother got
yelled at for being too rambunctious. We were suddenly
hiding in our rooms again like we did when we were young
children.

Aside from being extraordinarily annoyed by not singing
when Matt was home, I was a teenager and tried not to be
home or at least not out of my room. I got my own phone
line, answering machine, all to keep myself occupied. I
read the books I wanted to read in my room, prayed in
private the way I wanted to pray, with my circle of religious
relics like I did when I was little and needed a good grade. I
practiced my pageant walks for summer competitions (and
since no one was looking, my waves, which I would need
when I would certainly be crowned Miss Teen Maryland). In
the absence of anywhere to audition, my mother and I took
a great interest in the pageant circuit. She spent hundreds
of dollars on my dresses, hotel rooms and travel expenses
for me to continue to be on my path to "being famous."
During those times, drawn between the world of a teenager
and this other developing spiritual world, I amazingly felt
balanced.

I delved into the weird kid groups—the thespians
(actors), the hippies, the outsiders. I had multiple friend
groups. One day I would be watching a movie with the
average girls and in the next acting out a play at a boy/girl
sleepover. The following, watching a John Waters film.
These "outsiders" were my saving grace in high school.
When I moved to Maryland halfway through eighth grade,
someone decided to give me the nickname *Stupid Susan*.
The name spread like wildfire through the school with
almost no one being able to say my name without the
Stupid in front of it. It perplexed me having that name
since I was bored to pieces in all of my classes, as I was
much farther ahead in my Catholic school than in this

school. The only place I had difficulty was in art class where we were building on techniques I had no knowledge of, like lithographs. I had one teacher who looked like Mark Twain and taught eighth grade English. He was my only friend in that class and came to my defense when people were picking on me.

By the time Sophomore year of high school came around, the nickname was less, but the outright hatred people seemed to have for me was deeply seeded. I had no idea what I could have done to have this sense of abandonment and cruelty thrust upon me from my peers. I tried everything to regain some way to fit in. I joined (and quickly quit) track. I realized I did not like running, only jumping. I helped on the sidelines of Junior Varsity boys' lacrosse. I joined the cheerleading squad. I was in over ten clubs my first year of high school, quickly acclimated myself to the theatre department, and did everything I could think of to fit it. Needless to say, it only held back the cruelty from a chunk of the students. However, with the friends I did make, my confidence grew.

When I was a freshman, another outcast with short dread locked hair tried to sit with me. At the time, I only had one other person who would sit with me at lunch. You would have thought this would have been an upgrade. Instead, I shunned her, thinking that she would ruin my image more and bring about more bullying. She was a vegetarian. I thought she was so strange, despite my lack of meat eating and love of animals. By the time I was sixteen, I became a vegetarian for ethical reasons. I credit this lovely soul who in one lunch period, someone that I could not appreciate, gave me a gift that will last a lifetime. I think we are all mind-numbingly stupid in our middle and high school years.

A fellow student in my grade passed away in a drunk driving accident. A few weeks after he passed, there he was, in the corner of my room. While I could not see him, I saw with my third eye (a concept I knew nothing about at that time), white and blue light coming from the corner of my room. I knew it was him. He wanted to tell others he was all right, and oozed a sense of love.

I joined one of my best friends at the time to visit his family to offer our condolences. However, how does a teenage girl tell parents of their newly passed away son, *"I just saw your son in my room. He says he is fine and loves you very much."* You just can't do that.

My ability to control my dreams became stronger. I was able to escape the bad guy, stop my dreams when they got too scary and wake myself up. I learned later in life I was teaching myself lucid dreaming. Somehow my subconscious mind had access to this ability without book knowledge. Lucid dreaming is the ability to become aware of your dream state, make changes in your dream, and even pull yourself out of a dream completely or wake yourself up.

My training with Michael grew less, which was not a bad thing since my stepfather's born again Christian decision. While I didn't share with him my experiences, I knew better, at this time, to not even tell my mother. It would eventually leak to him.

CHAPTER 4

A Little Bit of Hope in Life

As was expected, I ran off to New York City within a few weeks of graduating high school. I needed to go home. I couldn't spend another moment in a place I considered to be the homeland of the *Stepford Wives*. My confidence was squashed. My home life became increasingly worse with my mother deepening in her depression, my stepfather losing his job, and my brother turning into a pot-smoking football jock.

I spent the summer living with one of my half-sisters from my father's first marriage, whom I had recently met. During my senior year of high school, my mother tracked down my half-sister, Claudia. She made arrangements with her for me to live with her.

I was excited to have a sister again. She spoiled me with getting my hair done at an expensive salon, told me to pluck my thick brown eyebrows, taught me about great shampoos, soap, and provided me with a job at her work.

A little while after I started at Marymount Manhattan College, a falling out occurred between my mother and Claudia that I only became aware of when I was being kicked out. I was yelled at, sworn at, and told to move out. Once again I had no idea what had transpired, other than my extended family didn't want to associate with my immediate family anymore, and that included me. I thought about everything I could have done wrong. I cleaned the house. I watched the cat. My mother sent me money to buy food. I was humble and thoughtful. I didn't know anyone to go out with. She had insisted I get out of the studio apartment more to meet people and enjoy the city. I spent most time alone as she was at work or with her boyfriend.

Fortune had made space for me in a dorm, well, a makeshift dorm. Marymount had rented space in several buildings in the city to use as dorms. I was staying at the YWCA. I moved into the dorms where I met lots of aspiring actors, fellow New Yorkers, and people from all walks of life. I started hanging out with a girl from the Bronx who went clubbing with me. I had a sweet friend, whom I snuggled with and watched *Mystery Science Theatre*. I befriended a southern towering black man, who within a month confronted me with a serious question. What would I think of him if he were gay? Needless to say, I wouldn't think anything different of him. After asking the question to several other people, our friend came out of the closet in full force! He already had a fashionable sense down to matching underwear to his clothes. Now he increased his height with platform shoes. I had someone to talk about guys with and I dove into the world of being a *fag hag* (girl who hangs out regularly with gay men).

With my new friends, I frequented gay bars, including Columbia University gay night, CBGB's gay night and more. I kissed guys my gay friends kissed. I danced without worrying about how much I was loved. My gay friends loved me for who I was. They were my family.

I also quickly found a Marymount favorite at the time— the Jungle Bar. At the Jungle Bar, I could hop onto the bar with my other freshman girlfriends and drink shots while dancing. The bartenders got to know me well, as this was my place of choice. During these short months, I had the time of my life going to as many bars as possible, kissing as many men as possible, having as many gay friends as possible, and overall running up as much debt as possible. While my confidence was being rebuilt, my grades suffered.

By the new year, I secured an internship at the Dramatists Guild through my playwriting professor. As part of my internship, I was blessed with his need to educate. I had to spend time during each visit reading plays and talking to him about them. I learned to file, answer phones and help prepare for play readings. I learned all the gossip about the playwrights, who was nice, who was a *queen,* and who was humble.

My favorite play was *Angels in America.* One day several playwrights gathered. Coming out of the elevator was Tony Kushner, the author of my favorite play. My heart stopped. Amid all of the celebrities I was seeing daily in New York City—from Liza Minnelli at my favorite diner to Robert De Niro on the street hailing a cab—this was the one that had me breathing into a paper bag while my friend and fellow intern laughed at me.

In May of 1995, I came back to Maryland where my mother was undergoing serious financial distress. I came home in debt with college loans, and with no money to return to school. In fact, I owed my school money for my dorm and I could not get a loan for another semester until that was paid off. I clearly did not have the resources to help me get back to college.

I quickly got a job as a receptionist in the building where my mother lived, and soon thereafter two other part-time jobs—one short-term in retail and one as a nanny to the cutest little boy.

I spent time with friends who did not go to college or attended one locally. I kept myself busy with dating to avoid the inevitable demise of my college education. I missed my New York friends. I missed my freedom. I missed my home.

The fall of that year, a man, who was a friend, and I started dating. I still don't know why I chose to date him. By that time two of his friends were seeking me out, another guy who lived in the same building was also pursuing me and I had been proposed to by a mason who was a part-time opera singer.

Kevin was 6'2—with dark hair and a solid body from working out—and withdrawn. He wasn't one for words except when watching sports, which was not something I was ever interested in. He worked at his family's welding business, hating every moment of it. He was a heavy drinker and certainly not a feminist like I was.

But our awkward partnership began. When you are a young woman dating, you have no clue what you need. You turn every moment that should cause alarm into a "that's

OK." He rarely paid for me when we went out. A bachelor, he never kept food in his house and would order food without asking me if I wanted to order anything. He wasn't kind, or giving. He was a Libra alpha male who had to be in charge and the smallest thing would throw him off. I remember meeting one of our mutual friends out. Jay told me he had feelings for me and what did I see in Kevin. I could not even explain it to myself yet.

On Valentine's Day a few months after we started seeing each other, we went to dinner at TGI Friday's and at the end of the evening, he said, "I love you." To avoid any awkwardness I said, "I love you," back. How does one know if they are in love with someone else? I asked this very question to one of my co-workers, who responded with if I had to ask that question, what does that tell me?

We broke up during the summer and one month later got back together. I felt alone and scared. After many apologies over who knows what, we were back together.

I spent a few days being sick during the month of August 1996. At first running a fever and vomiting profusely. Naturally I thought I had a stomach virus. While my period was never regular, I was a day late. Normally that would have never meant anything to me. I never took a pregnancy test before, but I felt something was different. I told Kevin what I thought and we bought a pregnancy stick. Within a few minutes the stick said I was pregnant. I felt sick to my stomach at the thought that I was pregnant. I was nineteen. I was not married. I had not finished college or had a career yet. We bought another one, only to have the same results. I scheduled an appointment with my gynecologist who ordered a blood test. After a few excruciatingly long few days, I had a call from the office nurse who confirmed I was pregnant.

After being in shock, Kevin and I knew we had to tell our parents. I did not look forward to telling my old school Catholic mother and his conservative Catholic parents the news. My mother freaked out and yelled and cried. "You have to get married." In the living room, never used in Kevin's parents' house, with them sitting in white, winged back chairs on white carpet with white walls staring me down, they yelled and finally concluded, "You have to get married." We both disagreed with our parents' decisions, but by Halloween, he proposed in a bag of candy and I accepted.

Over the next few months I continued to vomit all day, which was not easy with being a receptionist. Luckily I lived in a studio apartment in the building where I worked. The pre-natal vitamins made the nausea worse and I lost ten pounds, which concerned the doctors, especially with my slight frame.

One night I had a dream of a baby boy. He was missing some teeth. I told my mother this, and she said the teeth were a bad omen. In her family's traditions, losing teeth means death. Missing teeth is just bad.

However, a few months later the nausea subsided and I was eating everything under the sun. I became very strict with my pregnancy. I stopped coloring my hair blond, leaving awful dark brown roots. I stopped my luxury of scalding hot showers and cut out all caffeine. My mother advised me to eat lots of vegetables, something I was not a fan of. (I later learned I loved vegetables, just not squishy soft like my mother cooked them and not conventional raw vegetables—organic did not have that bitter taste.) I craved vegetables and fruits and ate them all day, every day. I also craved coffee. I was never one to crave coffee before, as I thought it was disgusting how my mother could not function in the morning without two cups, which immediately sent her to the bathroom and gave her bad breath. However, now, that was another thing I wanted so intensely. So, I allowed myself to sit in cafes and just smell them. (The thought of decaf did not even occur to me. I had pregnancy brain. Who can think clearly with that?!)

I had my sixth month sonogram and by then I was convinced I was having a girl. The sonogram confirmed it. I had always known. When I was a teenager, I had a feeling that when I was nineteen I was going to be raped and have a daughter. While I was not raped, I knew all about her. She was compassionate with oodles of passion. She was creative and dynamic. She had a great sense of humor and personality overall. My expected due date was in April, calling for an Aries. That was perfectly in sync with what I knew about her. All I can say was that I knew her before I "knew" her. It was just one of those unexplainable moments in my life I would later learn would be a normal thing for me.

As my belly swelled, the people in the building looked down on me—a knocked up single teenager. The guys I worked with were gentle and protective, yet sad for me. Midway through my pregnancy, Kevin and I moved in with his parents to save money. I did not drive so he and his mother drove me to work every day.

I threw myself into nurturing my little girl. I recorded me talking to her, singing to her and reading her stories like Dr. Seuss' *Drum Drum*. She would kick my belly in excitement when I put the headphones of the cassette player on my ballooned stomach.

Completely unaware of what pregnancy was like, I became obsessed with reading about her, my body and how to teach her when she was born. I bought books on baby sign language, development, and tried to figure out how to control the insatiable itching. Meanwhile the wedding was being planned for June, a few months after she was born.

Getting a wedding dress while you are pregnant is not easy. I decided to purchase a dress from the place I had my first job as a teenager. The owner was accommodating, but gave me the same despaired look everyone else did. Getting fitted for the dress and predicting how my body was and will be in early summer confounded them all. We did the best we could.

Meanwhile, Kevin and I argued over baby names. I always like different names like Yvonne and Isabella, while Kevin like traditional names like Michelle and Mary. The closest agreement we could come to was Jennifer. That was the only common name I could stand.

One day we were in the same room and suddenly walked over to each other. "Hope?" he said. "Hope," I said. We both got the name at the same time. Hope had named herself. That was what I had wanted. The middle name would be Alexandria. Kevin knew it would be a feminine version of my father's middle name. For me, it also had a connection to Alexandria, Egypt, although I did not know why that was important for me.

In my last month of my pregnancy, with little sleep, always peeing, and being uncomfortable physically, I did everything I could to induce labor. Earlier in the pregnancy, I was put on bed rest for a short cervix and possible miscarriage. However, with Kevin in school and always out with his friends, I had no one to help with laundry and cleaning. My doctor became rather upset with me at the time. Now inching towards the finish line, I was walking up and down steps, carrying laundry baskets, squatting and standing to no avail. For two weeks I walked around in labor. The pain was mild, I became ninety percent effaced and very dilated. I was seeing my obstetrician every two days who always ended our visits with, "I'm sure I will see you in the hospital in the next twenty-four hours."

After two weeks of never making it to the hospital, she decided it was time to schedule an induction. She had wanted me to hold off as long as possible because she was worried my daughter's birth weight would be too low since I only gained twenty three pounds. However, I was uncomfortable physically and more uncomfortable that we were moving towards a Taurus baby. I was not going to have a Taurus!

We scheduled an induction at the hospital a few days later on a Monday. She did not think I would last the weekend, but Monday morning, I came up to the hospital with Kevin, checked in and waited for her to arrive.

My obstetrician broke my water and within ten minutes, oh-my-god was I in labor! After a half-hour, obstetricians being obstetricians, they wanted to speed up the labor and gave me Pitocin. Being a young, first time mother, I trusted her and had no idea what that meant. What it meant was, "You think those were contractions before. Here comes the mother load!"

In my hospital bed wearing a cotton, oversized gown, I was connected to device after device. I was freezing cold and it was a pain to the nurses when I had to use the bathroom. Forget about asking for water, they only permitted me a few ice chips.

Kevin spent most of the time in the waiting room watching a game on the television with our families. I, alone in the room, felt a mixture of feeling like I was dying and wanting to die from the pain. There was a picture of Mother Mary in my room and having a relationship with her since I was young, I tried to focus on it.

The anesthesiologist was in another room with a mother delivering twins; so there was nothing they could do for me except give me Demerol to help subside the pain. The nurse was so annoyed with my pain and my not breathing properly she gave me the shot. "Didn't you go to birthing classes and learn how to breathe properly?" she asked condescendingly. I wasn't good at breath work at this point in my life. I always started hyperventilating when taught any kind of breath work. That continued until I was in my thirties.

Meanwhile I felt like I could see clouds and I was part of them, but the pain was still there and the Demerol made me nauseous. About one hour before I was to deliver, the anesthesiologist arrived, plugged me in and gave me relief. However, I was so out of it that I wound up needing an oxygen mask.

When it came time to push I could feel nothing and all I could do was assume I was pushing. They gave me an episiotomy to help her out. Soon slid out my little girl. She was moved to the plastic container in the corner where they tested her. She scored low, they believed she broke her shoulder since she did not move it, and did not cry at first. As she had her first bowel movement in the plastic basket in the corner, Kevin cried for joy (he hopped into the room when I got the epidural). They put her in a blanket, let me hold her for a minute and whisked her off into the NICU. I was cleaned up and sent to a room.

In that room I slept. I had the worst migraine I could ever have had, second degree swelling, and fought with the nurse about getting a catheter. Everyone seemed to think they knew what was best for me while I found myself having to stand my ground while I literally could not stand up. Kevin's mom wanted to keep my curtains open, but I could not stand the light with my migraine.

After the initial brief visits, all of our families—including Kevin—left me by myself once again.

The evening nurse brought another nurse in to examine me. She wanted to force me to have a catheter. One of the nurses who helped me go to the bathroom during the day told me that to help myself, I would have to do the following: a) void on my own regularly, b) have a bowel movement within twenty four hours, and c) start being able to walk. She also gave me the tip to press into my bladder with my fingers to help push out the urine. It worked.

I was never so determined, despite being extremely sensitive to medicine. By morning I hit all of those marks much to the chagrin of the nurse in charge. Walking however, was still an issue. Even though the epidural had worn off, I could not stand straight and my pelvic area was so inflamed every moment brought extreme pain.

By the next day I was wheeling myself to the NICU to see my daughter who was jaundice, hooked up to IVs, under a lamp, and being bottle-fed and given a nuk. When the lactation consultant came to help me nurse, Hope did not want to nurse. Since her first day on earth, that bottle was much easier than nursing. Why try harder?

After a few days I developed an infection and Hope was still in the NICU. We both nursed our illnesses in opposite sides of the hospital. The lactation nurse came in to berate me.

"Why is it you never see your daughter? Why are you not trying harder to breast-feed? Don't you want the best for her?"

In my mind, she called me a bad mother. Three days into it, I was awful at my new job. With no wheel chair, I held onto the poles along the wall, hunched over, I painstakingly went to go to Hope.

Later on when the lactation nurse came back, my emotions came pouring out. In a mix of tears and aggravation, I defended myself and told her I was not a bad mother and just because she did not see me going to visit her during the day does not mean I was not going. I dragged myself with no wheel chair there, having a fever of 103 degrees. She knew nothing.

The nurse was taken aback. The impact of her words to me had not registered in her head. I could tell she felt guilty, misunderstood, but I really did not care about that.

Well, actually I did, but did not want to deal with her guilt. She apologized. I reported her and the nurse from the first night to my obstetrician and the hospital. I was released soon thereafter.

Hope continued to have the hiccups all day long, which was no different than when I was pregnant with her. She was born at 7 lbs. 12 oz. and 21.5 inches long. She did not look like a newborn with her size and full head of black hair.

Kevin's mom doted on her. I grew jealous. She was my baby and I wanted to feed her, change her and bathe her. I saw a past life connection with them that I resented. It was only many years later that I came to understand Paula. She was the oldest of six children and helped her mother raise her siblings. She was a nurse. She only had sons. All of this was part of her natural skills. Plus, she had a little girl to spoil.

Kevin, who started culinary school while I was pregnant, focused on that. When he was not at school, he was out drinking with friends. I was at his parents' house, with no job, a new baby, no driver's license, and without a support system. A few months later, we married.

I was not blind in what I was doing. My bridesmaid and Kevin's mother all told me to change my mind. How can you possibly explain to someone that you need to do something that is temporary, because you know there is a karma that needs to be rectified? So, in a nearby Catholic church, I walked down the aisle in a very big, poofy, white wedding gown and exchanged vows in front of family and friends.

CHAPTER 5

Just Say Buddha

I had started working in a children's clothing store after my daughter was born to get a break. After a while, I realized I needed my own money, as the money I made at the store was just used to buy more clothes for my daughter. I started working at a doctor's office a few miles from my in-laws' home. An Indian woman, whom I saw several times a week when she brought her son in for special skin treatments, started telling me how when women leave a man, they need to make an exit plan, stowing away money, finding an attorney. I never mentioned to her about my newly bad marriage, but my unhappiness must have shown through. By then, Kevin and I were always fighting. If he wasn't in school, he was out drinking with his friends. And when he was home, he was bullying me and becoming physical. While I never was hit or punched or had furniture thrown at me like my mother, shoving pacifiers into my mouth to shut me up, pressing me into walls, and punching a hole in the wall when he was upset was still abuse. Even though I could recognize it, I thought perhaps these things were growing pains and he could change.

When the Autumn arrived, Kevin and I started making plans as to where he would do his internship. We both decided Florida, where it was warm. His parents were devastated by our decision. Meanwhile my mother was undergoing a divorce from husband number three and moved in with my father, who lived in the same building as my mother. In January of 1998, we packed a large U-Haul and went from snowy roads to the sun shining down on us.

As we acclimated to our new environment, I started delving into every book about religions I could get my hands on. If one day my daughter asked me what I believed in, I needed to have an answer.

I devoured books about Judaism, Buddhism, Kabbalah, and Hinduism. I found myself deeply connecting with Buddhist philosophy. However, did this mean I was a Buddhist? Part of me wanted to struggle with believing in only one religion, but I couldn't. However, I found myself on a path to discovering what I truly believed in.

In Amelia Island, I picked up a job as a freelance writer for *The News Leader* and worked at a doctor's office. Why the local paper took a chance on me I will never know. I was a flighty twenty-one-year-old with no computer. I would use a typewriter to write my stories, turning in a poorly written article late, which they would need to edit. I think I only had two assignments that I successfully had published. One was on kayaking where I had my first experience in one. I joined a beginner's training where we paddled through the marshes and were told how to flip our kayak all the way around because alligators might tip us over. Another was on a Cessna airplane that did local tours. I refused to enter the craft.

A few short weeks after I started at the doctor's office, Arabella entered my life. To make friends with me, you have to be in my face and say something interesting. I am not easy to make friends with. I could examine that for a million years and come up with many reasons, but they pretty much boil down to me being shy.

A few months after being at the doctor's office, Arabella became a receptionist there, also having just relocated to the area. Most water signs wiggle their way into your life until you suddenly realize they tricked you into opening up and friendship—Arabella was no exception. I remember her standing, one day, on my right side while I was seated and working. And while I was in work mode (heavily focused), leaning towards me, smiling, she was telling me something interesting. I think she may have mentioned Buddha, and you know there was no turning back from there. We spent enormous amounts of time together talking about science, religion, history, philosophy, and astrology. She was already an extremely gifted self-taught astrologer at the time and got me even more sucked in.

Arabella's husband was a chef and they had recently moved to Amelia Island from Virginia for his work. She ignited my mind, my spirit and my imagination. She was the biggest influence in my life at the time, my best friend and my teacher. She introduced me to the concept of past lives, which fit perfectly for me. It made many of my life experiences up until now make sense.

I never felt like my parents were my parents. From my earliest memories, I had this feeling that I was somewhere I was not supposed to be for many years. I did not know how to vocalize it. One day as a young child I finally figured out what was wrong.

"You are not my mother and he is not my father," I said in a matter of fact tone to my mother.

My mother laughed. "Of course we are!"

"No you are not. You are not my mother and he is not my father," I said again. And while I was making a statement, there was part of me looking for an explanation.

"I have pictures of me pregnant with you. Do you want me to show you?" My mother asked, now probably thinking I thought I was adopted or stolen.

"The pictures won't matter," I replied. In my mind I thought they could have been doctored, but I did not tell her that.

We had this conversation a few times more until I wore on my mother's nerves. After that I stopped bringing it up, but she never stopped showing me pictures of her pregnant.

One time in Catholic school, a teacher was leading my class down the stairs to our next class. I was a tremendously klutzy child; even falling up the steps, so changing classrooms was always a bother to me. We were held up between a set of steps when in my head I grew frustrated with myself.

"I used to be much taller than this," I said in my mind. I could feel this tall lanky male body that was an energetic version of me, which was nothing like my short child self. "My arms don't work right in this body!"

These were some of the things that ran through my mind growing up, which included a complete disassociation and distaste for the process of eating and voiding. All I could think of was how this was a disgusting process and I did not want to be part of it.

I also found myself deep in prayer as a child. I would sit on my bed and surround myself in a circle with every Catholic artifact I had, praying the rosary, for a good report card. However, often I would just pray out of piousness. One time in my bedroom I saw a white orb floating towards my headboard. It hung out for a brief few seconds until I acknowledged it. It then moved into the headboard and disappeared into the wall. When I was grown I mentioned this to my mother, who confirmed the story and said, "Don't you remember? You always used to say you saw and talked to angels in your room and Mary."

Yep, I must have been a weird child. Which begs the question, who was my mother to be such an accepting person and not squelch these experiences? My mother did not believe in past lives, but she did have a firm grasp of intuition and the other side from her family.

My mother's knowledge of "the other side" was limited along with the vast ways to communicate with it. However, she did believe that the women in her family all were "gifted." When women turned thirteen, they would inherit the gift of vision through dreams. What we all didn't know at the time was that I was a walking intuitive. Arabella understood all of this and nurtured it in me, and nurturing of any kind was needed at the time.

When Kevin abruptly decided to quit his job, we needed a Plan B. He had continued his role of being completely absent in our lives, choosing to drink with his new friends rather than be home (and when he was home, no one was happy).

I thought perhaps if we went back North, we could be close to his parents for babysitting, but far enough away from his friends. I sent him on a trip to job hunt. By October 1998, we moved to Pennsylvania.

In York, we were forty-five minutes away from his parents. I found a job working at a catering company. He worked several jobs until he settled at Fed Ex. I started thinking about how this marriage was going nowhere fast. When he was home, he had rules that a Sagittarius like me found restricting. Rule one—do not pay any attention to anything (book, magazine, child) when he is in the same room with me. I had to focus solely on him working out or what game he was watching on television. Rule two—do whatever he wants and all will be well. I spent years being told how I was unattractive, useless, and horrible at many things. He was obsessed with blond, short hair and one time pinned me down threatening to cut off my hair when he was upset with me.

A little while after Hope was born, I learned to drive. I was supposed to get my license when I was sixteen, but my mother grounded me for something small and I was not allowed. When I left high school, I didn't need a license in NYC. When I moved back to Maryland, it didn't occur to me, as I lived in the same building as I worked. During the beginning of our relationship I depended on him and his mother for rides. However, that was no longer an obstacle for me. But what was holding me back? I loved change. I needed to change my furniture around the house to keep sane. (A sign of someone who clearly moved around a lot.) I was not ready. So, I found refuge in yoga at a nearby recreation center. I was fantastic at balasana, also known as child's pose. You start on all fours, sink back onto your heels and melt into a ball of yourself. I think that was probably the only asana I truly paid deep attention to during the first few years of doing yoga.

Kevin and I decided to buy a house and save on rent. We looked at few homes until we decided on a duplex about five minutes from where we were living. The duplex was approximately two hundred years old. When we toured the house with the real estate agent, I felt a presence follow me as we walked up staircase after staircase. I felt the energy of a woman, felt the coolness of her touch, and heard the name Maria.

I asked the real estate agent who "Maria" was and how she was here with us as we toured the house. Needless to say the agent was either freaked out and attempting to hide it or thought I was crazy, as she stopped talking to me and from that moment on, talked to Kevin.

A few short weeks after moving into the house, we received a letter addressed to the former occupant who passed away—Marie. I spent time trying to send Marie to the light, imagining her in my mind and this vortex of light leading her up to heaven. I had no experience in this area and was unsuccessful. So, I prayed for her to move on. One day when I went upstairs to the attic—which was converted to my daughter's playroom—where she seemed to be the most, she was no longer there. I had a dream soon thereafter that a young woman took her hand and they went off together.

I did however feel a male presence in the house. He loved to hang out in our bathroom or in my daughter's room, which connected to the bathroom. Any opportunity he had to be a prankster and trip men in our house when they needed to go to the bathroom, he did. It took me a few instances to put two and two together as I could not see him or any ghost at the time. However, after a while it was too coincidental to discount. There wasn't a guy who entered that house who didn't trip once heading towards the bathroom. Women seemed to be exempt.

CHAPTER 6

The Pirate Luc

Soon after I moved into my new home I became immersed at New Visions, a holistic bookstore near my home. I started attending their "Friday Night Forums," where holistic topics were discussed. Topics ranged from astrology to angels to tarot readings by one of the owners, Bill, a sturdy built bald man with the most unique way of being straightforward yet gentle. The store was filled to the brim with like-minded, New Age-minded folks. I loved the talks, the vanilla cream sandwich cookies, and the array of people I met there. I became entrenched in this place and started taking a Tarot certification workshop. Soon after Tarot were Self-Mastery classes where we talked about money, relationships, goal planning, life maps and more.

In Tarot class we learned in-depth knowledge of the Rider Waite deck. Our small group learned and practiced on each other, soon branching out to doing reading for family and friends. Arabella, who already was a novice at Tarot, guided me when I had questions.

In 2001, I needed to see my friend, Arabella, once more in person. Phone conversations and letters were great, but I needed to hug my friend. Arabella and Mark were still living in Amelia Island so I planned a visit. It takes a lot of love to get me on a plane. As a child, I had experienced heavy turbulence, an almost emergency landing and air masks dropping down. She joked I needed to go get a sedative from my physician, but instead I stayed awake for twenty-four hours so on the plane all I needed was sleep.

"Afraid of planes?" inquired a gentleman sitting across from me.

"How could you tell?" I asked.

"You had it written all over your face. Glad you slept."

Arabella and her husband, Mark, picked me up from Jacksonville Airport and we drove to her home, which I had been in many times before. She lived in a townhouse apartment surrounded by marshes, very typical of that area. When we got settled, we were both in the kitchen while she opened a bottle of wine for us.

"What is that clicking?" I asked her.

"What clicking?"

"It sounds like a cricket."

She did not hear it, but responded, "could be." And then it was silent. Within a few minutes, the sound started up again.

"OK. Now it sounds like it is going from the kitchen to the living room and back and forth."

At this point, I think she thought I needed to have my hearing checked or at the very least, my ears were funny from the plane.

We walked from the kitchen to the living room nearby and sat while the noise continued. Later that evening, Mark, being the great chef he is, made a four-course meal that was completely wasted on me (being such a picky eater at the time). After dinner, Mark disappeared to give us girl time as we sat in the living room.

A figure like a black shadow stood at the edge of the kitchen island looking my way. Freaked out is not a word that could even cover how I felt at the time. As a kid, I saw balls of light, and angels. I felt the presence occasionally of people who passed on or from my home in York, felt a ghost's presence, but that was it. I was never able to see a ghost or someone who crossed over with my two eyes and yet there he was.

I started asking Arabella in a tentative voice, "Do you see that?"

"What?"

"The dead guy standing right there?"

And with that, Arabella passed it off as if nothing was different in the room. After all, she believed in ghosts and the subject was so nonchalant to her.

Mentally, I was completely losing it and to boot, he decided to make physical contact. I felt him wrap his fingers around my neck. And I lost it.

The clicking was him, obviously seeing something in me that meant I could be aware of him. My hearing the clicking acknowledged to him he could try to make contact. His showing me himself was another test of, "Can you see me," and when I could, his touch was not only a "Can you feel me," but a "Hey, I have a story to tell you."

He then showed me a young man in a bathroom. He wore a plaid shirt and jeans. He guided me into this vision like a tour and then took the place of the actor. On the shower railing was a rope, and then he stepped his head into it telling me he either killed himself or was hung.

Mark and Arabella had a little girl, who was spending time with Arabella's aunt, Diane. My bed was the twin size bed in the nursery, where I stayed up for a good portion of the night with him staring at me and me praying him away with Our Fathers and Hail Marys. When I woke up in the middle of the night to him still there, I went downstairs to the living room, put on the television for distraction, and watched TV until dawn. I curled up into a ball and tried focusing on TV shows and my prayers. Did I mention he stayed staring at me all night long?

The next morning, I started to feel safer with the sun up. I know that must sound ridiculous, but in the night, all I could feel was this ominous presence around me. In the sunrise, I felt comfortable enough to go back to the room and sleep. When I woke up again, Arabella was still sleeping, and I headed for the shower only to have him hanging out trying to talk to me. I ignored him, feeling more empowered by the sun (and probably too sleepy to worry so much).

He kept pushing the story he showed me the night before putting into it a twinge of murder. He showed me blood on the bathtub and as if there were other people involved, but not involved. I could not make out what was the true story.

I told Arabella everything that happened the night before. "We should send him to the light," she said.

"Uhm, no. I don't know how to do that. I don't know if I can or if I want to," I replied getting scared at the thought of engaging this man.

We sat in her dining room with the chandelier light on, playing twenty questions with this dead guy. With each question, the lights would dim or light up on their own.

Later on that Saturday evening we went to hang out on her bed and do a Tarot reading. Shortly after the reading, he came back and was on me like a moth to a light bulb. My hair stood on end. I tried explaining this butterfly-like feeling that was vibrating all around my skin. "He is on top of me! He is touching me." And I think Arabella thought I was a wuss until she put her hands on my hands to stop me from shaking out of my skin. Then she immediately felt him and exclaimed, "Oh my God!"

"I told you!"

"Let's say the Hail Mary for protection," Arabella, a former Catholic, spat out.

As we said our prayers, I felt this deep blanket of love and protection come over me. I started to feel as if I was levitating. When I opened my eyes, Arabella was staring at me. "Did you feel that?"

"Yep," she calmly said.

"I feel like I am not even in my body right now."

"Cool, huh," she replied. "Now, let's send him to the light."

Despite my whining about not knowing how, she told me to stay in this relaxed space and try and visualize. I saw this ray of white and golden light come down to the right side of the wall where Arabella was. We both told him to go to the light and eventually I became quieter seeing him in this vortex of light. Mentally I kept telling him and praying for him to move on. He would edge up the vortex, stop and then out of fear try to get away from this pulling force of nature. Over and over this cycle would continue, even with angels reaching their arms for him to follow them. And then after a while, he was exhausted, I was exhausted and we both knew he wasn't going anywhere tonight.

"I am sleeping with you and Mark tonight," I said blankly to Arabella.

Cuddled up to her, even with his eyes on me, I slept. That night I had a dream that she and I signed a contract. When I shared this with Arabella the next day, she asked me what we promised we would do for him. I couldn't remember, but we soon both realized we promised to help him cross over to the other side.

When I was leaving to go home, I told her she needed to find out if a young man committed suicide in that apartment or the neighboring ones. To no avail, she could not find a man who committed suicide in the area.

Arabella spent years dealing with him trying to communicate through physical actions. She woke up one evening with him in her room, solid as could be, thinking at first they had an intruder. One time, he placed fingers on her throat as if to choke her. After the latter, she called in Archangel Michael and asked for his help in removing this ghost from her home. By the next day, he was gone.

Many years later, she discovered who this haunting man was—Luc Simone Aury. Said to haunt the old jail on Amelia Island, Aury was the son of a pirate, and had his fair share of horrid crimes. Sentenced to hang, he slit his own throat. That however did not stop his executors who stitched him up and hung him for good measure. When Arabella moved to Tampa, after having looked at an empty house before renting it, she found pennies on the floor move-in day. "Pennies from heaven," she thought. She knew Luc was saying hello.

CHAPTER 7

Beacon for Dead People

When I arrived home from my visit with Arabella, I felt like I was going mad. I could see, hear and feel ghosts all around me. While I had a connection to the other side previously, this was new territory. Before they were happy, loving spirits. Now they were loud, confused, and needed to get their point across.

After the freaky experience, I needed someone who could help me work through my currently panicked state. My mind was suddenly a flashing beacon calling in every dead person in the tri-state area looking to talk to their loved one. All I wanted to do was climb under the covers. They did not seem to understand this.

Within two days of being back from visiting Arabella, I started flipping through the Yellow Pages. What do you search for? An exorcist? A holistic support group for those going insane? I flipped category after category knowing I was completely at a loss. I suddenly felt guided to go to the section on "Hypnotherapy." I knew very little about hypnotherapy, although more than the concept that they could make you walk around and squawk like a chicken.

I first used my mind to pick a person, which led to an answering machine. Could not leave a message about this. Next, I used my intuition to guide me to a name. I had no time to waste. On the other end, Lucille answered.

"Hi. I think I need to make an appointment, but I have no idea if you can help me. Would you tell me what kind of people you work with?" I asked timidly.

With her soothing voice, Lucille, persisted in me telling her what I might need help with. She invited me to tell her in a very gentle way.

"Do you ever do anything with holistic type of stuff," I asked.

"Yes," she replied and persisted for details.

"Well, do you ever deal with ghosts?" I put everything on the line there. While my mind was reasoning she was going to think I was a quack and hang up, she simply said yes and we should meet.

In a blur of a few minutes, I gave her the details of my experience. She laughed a soft, comforting laugh and I knew she could help me. In fact, something told me that the moment she picked up the phone.

Lucille made room in her calendar for me the following week. While I felt I could not possibly wait a whole week, my financial situation was precarious at best and a week gave me time to save money.

Meanwhile back in my dining room that I was painting a cobalt blue was a Jamaican woman who kept yelling at me to call her daughter. I tried getting the numbers right from her, but after two days of a wrong combo of phone numbers, she gave up on me and left.

The day of my appointment I drove to downtown York, to a section I had not been to before. It was decayed and felt strange. What felt stranger was that as soon as I parked the car and stepped onto the street, I had an invisible visitor walking with me, side by side.

Lucille's office was in her home, an old row home like most in the area. As soon as I stepped inside, the odd feeling of the air outside dissipated and was replaced by pure Zen.

To the left of the entrance was her office, which would have been a living room. She had plants, comfy chairs, soft blankets and soothing sounds from the water fountain. I sank into the chair, wrapped the blanket around me protecting my fragile mind.

The first few sessions, spaced two weeks apart, focused on getting me calm and relaxed. After that we moved onto learning to control my beacon and standing my ground when unwanted visitors would persist. That was not easy.

Imagine trying to retrain yourself from a lifelong habit. Multiply that by ten and that's how hard it was for me. In my mind I could now see, hear, taste, feel everything in this world and beyond and "they" did not care if I was busy or scared.

During the first couple of weeks, I mentioned to Lucille (who I found out was also intuitive), about my visitor who comes with me every time I see her.

"I know," she exclaimed. "Who do you think it is?"

"I have no clue," I said despondently.

She started having me honing my intuition to connect with him. What I did know was that it was a "he."

After only getting colors and emotions and a few intentions, she helped me out and introduced him to me as my spirit guide. Spirit guides are those from the other side who guide us in our daily lives, kind of like best friends who have only the loving intentions for you.

It took many months of training to feel comfortable with my guide, but after a while, I could see him more clearly and felt happy when he was around. I felt lonely in my day-to-day life, so this was a welcome relief.

My marriage continued to plummet with Kevin never home, always drinking, while I worked full time and cared for our young daughter. When he was home, it was the same old paying attention to only him, although I was starting to find the strength to go against the grain and do my own thing, but never without an ear full.

As I continued to hone my abilities, Lucille started delving into my new interest—past lives. As soon as I knew she could do this, I was hooked and ready to know more.

She prepped me through free writing, which was frustrating. On the first go with past life regression, I saw myself looking like Robin Hood in a forest, bow in hand. I could not press on after a few minutes. We played with time and angle and soon I could not feel anything but people rushing towards me. I believe they were going to kill me.

I came out of the experience chalking it up to my mind creating stories (along with my need for archery which was first recognized in high school). The "memory" was not crystal clear, nor did I feel a connection to it. But, we pressed on.

On the next regression, I saw myself as a little girl with super blond curls holding a man's hand. I knew he was my father in that life and I loved him more than anything in the world. I wore a purple velvet-like dress and we walked hand in hand down an aisle that looked like church pews with a red velvet carpet guiding the way. Later in the session I saw him sitting in a large wooden chair in a cement-like room. I climbed onto his lap to the chagrin of my mother, whom I recognized in my heart as my mother-in-law, Paula, in this life. I left that session knowing something was wrong. I longed to be with him again.

In another session I saw myself as the same girl, but slightly older, getting dressed as my mother treated me like a disease. My father was dead. Years had passed. Life was sad.

On the advice of Lucille, I continued to do free writing. After my Robin Hood session, I saw and wrote about seeing red velvet, feeling loved, and when I had the experience of me and my father I knew that was the bigger memory, as if like taffy, it was pulled and stretched out.

Once you open Pandora's Box, everything comes out. I started to remember with such vigor. When I was a child, I was obsessed with Egypt. I did not know why. After these sessions, I had a vision of standing on a wide stone patio space in Egypt, looking out at the sunset in the desert. In subsequent visions, I saw myself in my room being sad, once again, while someone brushed my hair for me. In another, I was with a cat who I recognized as my cat in this lifetime, Bella. And another where my husband was standing in my room near an entrance. I recognized him as my brother in this lifetime and all of that sadness made sense to me and that karma rolled over into this one. He was not the nicest person to me in that lifetime.

I believe that children have this inherent knowing. However, our reality does not match theirs. Most times parents brush off their children's comments as passing acts of imagination. I believe memories carry over, some clear, some clouded, but they struggle with the thoughts of previous lives.

When my daughter was two, before I met Lucille, we were sitting at the dining room table. I was working on something while she was scribbling away, crayons on printer paper. She paused and said, "I am sorry you died in that fire, mommy." After another moment of looking down, she continued to color.

"Thank you for saying that," I told her. We had never talked about past lives before. She was two. Our conversations revolved around Elmo, Blue's Clues and Little Bear. She was right, though. I had a vision for years I could not understand of being trapped inside a church on fire with my mother from this life. We, with the others, banged on the stained glass windows. I could see the grass outside the church and the little picket fence yards away. I had forgotten about this "memory" of mine until she mentioned it.

As I continued with Lucille, I saw myself as a gentleman wearing a suit, standing at a curb pulling out a pocket watch. With a gentleman's stick in hand, I took a step and could go no further. Over and over again we tried to make me walk across the street to no avail. Lucille, knowing what happened next, asked me to skip ahead five minutes. I saw myself dead on the cobblestone street hit by a car. I knew this was New York, and the car looked like it was from the time cars were being invented—huge behemoth black beasts.

Another time I saw myself as a gypsy toddler living in the woods. My mother was doing laundry and I was occupying myself playing happily. White men came into the forest and killed many. I was hung from a tree. Lucille and I did something very interesting next. I was so sad for my mother. I needed to comfort her. So, like a shamanic journey, we crossed time and space to tell her I was OK and that I loved her. I do believe that in that lifetime, she saw my spirit and it brought her peace.

I became so in awe of what Lucille could do with the mind. I continued my practice on my own and had another major revelation: the thought of me being raped and pregnant at nineteen. It was part real and part memory. Naturally, I was pregnant at nineteen with Hope, but there was no rape. Only consensual sex. However, I remembered being raped on stone ground by a soldier in a past life. I leaned against a building wall, thinking I was going to die. Instead, I had a little girl, my Hope in this lifetime. And the soldier was Kevin.

Having felt the karma that needed to be resolved was now uncovered, I sought to rectify anything I could. I created boundaries, but also opportunities for forgiveness, whether he was aware or not.

One evening, Kevin was chatting online with a woman. He was talking about them partaking in sexual activities. That was the moment I needed. I seized it. I told him to leave, like I did hundreds of times before, but this time he did. Perhaps he was ready, too.

My mother came to live with my daughter and me for a few weeks so we could get acclimated. I was working at a local PBS/NPR station, but with my hours, I could not get home in time to pick her up from school, so I secured after school care.

Hope and I started our first year of being just the two of us in the most raw, painful way. But we did it. We got out of a toxic situation. I was sure to never make that mistake again.

CHAPTER 8

Down at the River

A short while after Kevin moved out, I started going to a holistic center in Harrisburg that was run by a beautiful Japanese-born woman, Karen. At Millennium Health one could learn meditation, reiki, and more. I joined lunchtime meditation when I could. My first event there was a Shamanic Journey lead by a remarkable shaman. At the workshop I noticed a beautiful man with a gentle personality, great smile, and who sounded like a recovering pothead. Before I left, rather than finding him, I was befriended by a massage therapist named Missy who had a brown pixie cut and was pregnant with her third child. While Taurus' don't generally come off as the extroverted type, like most of my friends, she initiated the contact.

Missy was living with her boyfriend Jonas in York and had also made the half-hour trip to see Ms. Rice. We quickly became friends and I continued my search for how to see this mystery man again. After many other events at Millennium Health, one day, I finally met him—Tom. Tom had a house on a river in a rather remote and beautifully rustic area. His parents lived next door and he always had a flood of roommates. And he was single. Tom started to invite me over to hang out with many other people from the center. I felt so comfortable with Tom and he was a welcome rescue from my recent separation. It was wonderful to have someone to flirt with me! I felt needed and wanted, which was a feeling I had not experienced in over five years.

One day, Tom invited me over, just me, to hang out. While it was quite awkward at first trying to figure out what to say, Tom and I had lots of fun talking about spirituality. The next time we hung out, which I thought was going to be solo, I was met with another woman there, Stella. After hanging out, we all awkwardly sat on the floor of a spare room where there were only mattresses on the ground and candles. After a few hours and signs that Stella was going nowhere, I left. My gut told me something was wrong there... she was competition. My mind only thought about how Tom was the new partner in my life, despite no attempt from him to kiss me. But, what did I know? I had not dated another person since 1995, when everyone was learning how to date like adults.

Several weeks later I started noticing Tom becoming less physical. No more kisses on the cheek. Short hugs with pats on the back. These were not good signs. And he started pushing me towards a Capricorn spiritual bookstore owner who was in his forties.

When the weather was nice one day, Tom decided he was going to have a sweat lodge. Many of us who hung out at the river had never participated in one before so we were excited. Tom's parents offered to babysit my daughter, Hope, next door. Sweat lodges are an enclosed area where there is a pit in the middle you occasionally pour water over to create an extreme heat and steam to release the toxins in your body and mind. While traditional natives may have gone for hours in them, we decided to take breaks outside and get wet in the river to cool down so that none of us passed out. What I didn't know was the bare minimum rule. Yes folks, you get buck-naked! I could not do it. The trick was that you could get wet in the river and coat yourself with lots of mud, which also helped with the sweat lodge. I put my braved self forward, mostly trying to impress Tom with not being a prudish wimp, kept my underwear on, caked myself in mud and joined the group. Most of the guys kept their underwear on, as well.

After about two hours in the sweat lodge, Tom and Stella told me I was a great person, but that Tom decided to date Stella. My instincts were right.

"We wanted to tell you here among friends so we could all support you," said Stella.

My heart plummeted. I felt dizzy and nauseous and could not breathe. I could not understand what happened and why I was being told while so vulnerably naked, detoxing, and around others. It was embarrassing!

I rushed out of the sweat lodge after a few minutes realizing I could not be here now. I could not cry around these people. I ran inside, quickly washed off mud as best as I could, put clothes on and went next door to get my daughter who was playing with Tom's nephew and mother.

His father looked at me trying to see what was wrong. Everyone tried to get me, telling me it was OK. They just could not understand that after coming from a marriage that was completely hopeless, I thought I found love in just a few short months. My expectations were crushed.

After another few months of everyone calling me trying to get me to come back to the river, back to Millennium Health, back to friendship, I returned Karen's call asking to talk to her. I needed help putting myself back together again.

One Saturday in January, she sat with me in a small room at the center, walls covered in burgundy latex paint, listening while I said I was a broken teacup that could not be repaired. Karen, who was an amazing friend, became motherly with her soft words of "One day it will be better." Knowing I could not hear that at the moment, she simply listened and I am sure did a little Reiki on me.

After many, many months, I sucked up my pride and my heartbreak and went back to the River. By then Stella was living with Tom and my thoughts of how this doe-eyed woman who feigned innocent love started to melt away. Stella was genuine. You could not look into her pools of blue eyes and not feel loved. Her soft demure nature reminded me of Mary from Little House in the Prairie. She was caring, gentle, and loved to experiment with vegetarian food for our potlucks at the river. She was a gem, and Tom had been wise enough to see it. After learning more about Stella, I soon fell in love with her, too.

CHAPTER 9

Sometimes Life Leads You to a Buddhist Temple

Tom and Stella's home was a revolving door to deeply spiritual people who came to their potlucks, music sessions, and meditations at their home. They also always had incredible roommates. There was Rhonda from Alaska who had the greatest personality and had no qualms with being in a sweat lodge butt-naked and then caking herself in mud, a flamboyant guy with great hair who just loved everyone, and a Buddhist man who struggled with alcoholism and used to yell at us "young kids" to not run up the stairs, but take every step with measure and consciousness. And then there were those who came in and out to visit and call this our community second home.

Karen, Tom, Stella, and a few others were at the river house one day in a surprisingly adventurous mood. Tom and Stella had recently acquired a beat up van from the 80's whose back seats were ripped out. You could hear this sucker from a mile away... easily. And on one spring morning, we decided our adventure was going to NYC. We had no plan, just the gumption to go.

We arrived in Battery Park and decided it was a good place to park and poke around. While I grew up in NY, I had not been back to visit since 9/11 happened. We walked over to where the land was still being dug up and a steel fence like I have around my home wrapped around. There were meager signs indicating where we were while other ones with implicit "Do Not Cross."

I stood at the fence looking to feel something: sadness, longing, fear, or the souls of those who had been there. All I felt was emptiness. Those that passed away that day were not there (or at least did not present themselves to me). They moved on to the life beyond earth.

We decided to continue walking around and happened upon a Buddhist temple, feeling drawn to that building. Being the newly adventurous type, we decided to go in. I, being the most unadventurous person, would never have had the guts to go inside, but luckily I was with brave souls.

When we got inside, there was no one around. After a few moments, we were surrounded by greetings and invitations to a fire ceremony that was about to begin. We had no idea what was happening and were quickly ushered in with people giving up their seats for us. The two-hour ceremony began. There was a clear, glass, enclosed case about two feet tall standing near the front of the room. While we could not understand a word of what was being said, kind attendees near us took turns interpreting all being said.

After the ceremony, there were bows and we said our thanks. The monks led us to the main entrance to happily show us their home. I remember it being filled with lush burgundy fabrics and gold deities. The monks were so full of joy. They asked us if we wanted to be baptized Buddhist. Without a moment's hesitation we all looked at each other and said, "yes."

The ceremony took less than fifteen minutes and felt so sacred and still. The essence of this place could fill you with nothing other than a deep sense of inner peace. We were all quickly presented with certificates and a phone number if we wanted to train in Buddhism. We all received new names, although not knowing the language, were unable to interpret them.

While I was a grown woman with a child of my own, my mother, a stanch Catholic, went straight into mother mode, upset by what had transgressed with her daughter. I visited my mother a few days after my NY adventure, excited to share this incredible story, of a temple I never knew was in a city I grew up in, and showcase my certificate. My horrified mother pleaded with me saying I could not have done this because I was baptized Catholic. She told me not to forget God, and what a good religious child I was (a conversation she dictated to me many times over the years).

While I was incredibly enamored with Buddhism for many years, I knew that I could call myself Buddhist, but in my heart, could not be one. I was in my phase of a) the grass is always greener on the other side, b) all religions had too strict a dogma I could not confine myself to, and c) I could not rectify my beliefs to any religion in particular. All I knew at this point in time of my life was that there was a God, I was uncomfortable with the concept of God, I did not know everything, I did not believe every religion's story, and I was feeling my way through spirituality based on my experiences.

As anyone who has a spiritual side and unsure of what religion is right for them, I wanted to know about all of them. When my daughter was born, I started on a religion study bonanza. I decided that I needed to figure out what I believed in so one day when she asked, I could tell her. As age crept in, I slowed down my need to know everything instantaneously. I realized more each day that it was alright to not know.

Not long after our trip, Tom and Stella were married. They asked me and a few others to be bridesmaids in the wedding. I was very excited, as I had only been an adult flower girl in one of my aunt's Albanian weddings, which entailed me standing there at the house before the wedding started looking nice and people giving me compliments and money.

Tom and Stella's wedding at the river was simple and full of friends and family. Us bridesmaids did nothing special, just wore really cool Tibetan shirts and enjoyed the crowd. One night before the wedding I felt inspired to paint. I made a really archaic colorful painting and gave it to them as a wedding gift. They were kind enough to hang this painting, which I am sure looked like crap. They were able to see through the imperfections of my skills to see my heart was full of joy for them.

Karen became my new teacher. With her, I received my Usui Reiki training, which she taught in traditional oral style. When people ask me what Reiki (energy work) is like, I tell them to think about the dead of winter, in the dark, when it's so dry and you go to adjust your covers and you get shocked, seeing a speck of light. Humans are great electrical conduits. We may not see the energy move as we cannot see radio waves, but hear the radio. This energy, known as "Chi" in Asian cultures, surrounds us, moves through us. If our energy is off, it can cause physiological issues in the body. For example, if you are stressed, you might get a cold. We are all made of light. Energy runs through us: every atom and molecule. A Reiki practitioner receives the hands-on training and energy "attunements" (downloading energy from the other side) to be able to be the conduit to provide energy healing to others. A Reiki practitioner is not the electricity coming out of the socket or the plug you would put in. We are simply the funnels for God or the universe or the other side to bring light into your body to provide an adjustment for any issues you may be having.

Inspired by Lucille, I also studied Hypnotherapy and then NLP (Neuro-Linguistic Programming), which was conveniently available at New Visions. While my pocketbook suffered greatly, my soul was enriched. I now had a profession as a hypnotherapist. I called my business "Blue Lotus Studio."

I started renting a space with a sound therapist, Lana, who rented to me on a very temporary and inexpensive basis. Lana's office was large with a wicker loveseat and coffee table and adjoining chairs. In another section, she had set up a massage table for her work with instruments lining the area. Using the table and chairs, I did Tarot readings for people.

I had a talent for giving intuitive readings by this point, which evolved through my work with Lucille and my classes with Bill at New Visions, but no one wanted to see a young twenty-something-year-old girl scare them with knowing about their private life without them saying a word. So, I used Tarot as a means to provide a comfortable

space. My ego also appreciated it as I had honed the
confidence of relying solely on my intuition.

After about six months, Missy was looking for a space
to do massage and had soon moved with us. The basement
was not used and her boyfriend, who worked in
construction, offered to help turn it into a functioning
office for the both of us, if Lana was amenable. It took
several months and portable heaters during the winter to
get the space ready. Missy did massage. I did
hypnotherapy, past life regression and Reiki. And we soon
started offering Reiki classes for children.

Like most business owners, you have to really invest
incredible doses of time, energy and money. Being a single
parent, I could not offer much of any of those
requirements. And much to the chagrin of my teacher, I
had a difficult time charging people money, or at least a
decent amount for my services. Most times I offered them
for a donation. After a short time after Missy and I began in
our new basement office, I fizzled out, and Missy, with
three children, did, as well.

CHAPTER 10

No Peace Until You Know Peace

In the fall of 2003, I heard about his Holiness the Dali Lama coming to New York's Central Park for a public talk on compassion and a peaceful mind. He was last in New York in 1999 and now making his way back to bring a semblance of peace to the unsettled minds of Americans who just experienced a massive terrorist attack two years prior. Those organizing the event were looking for quite a number of volunteers as his last talk in the park garnered approximately two hundred thousand people. I did not hesitate in putting in an application to be part of this momentous weekend.

My application was approved and I was assigned to be at one of the many gates of Central Park with a few other volunteers. Upon arrival, we were given official tour t-shirts and hats to designate us as volunteers. We were instructed that Central Park would be open for general activities like rollerblading and biking, with those people allowed inside. Those who came for the talk, needed to present their pass for the free event.

At noon the talk started, but not without instructions letting us volunteers know that the park was now at capacity and anyone who wanted to join would be unable to do so. How hard would that be? Peaceful people coming to see a talk on peace. Much to my surprise, the atmosphere changed.

I find that being in large groups of people, even ten or more people can be overwhelming for me. I start to feel each person's feelings, which can even be the emotions behind a passing thought. We think of thoughts as just thoughts that come and go, but for me (I learned many years later), hang out like a cloud in the air until it decides to disperse or travel elsewhere. Thoughts with moderate or strong emotions can hang in the air for five, ten or even twenty minutes. So, there I am in a multitude of emotion unable to find my way out. I feel their pain, their anger, their anxiety. People had taught me many ways to "shield" myself, to grow a thick skin, but for me, I chose to rarely utilize these tools. My fear was that if I allowed myself to incorporate them, I would not be as compassionate and understanding. I already had so many shells, so many self-protective mechanisms that were inherent, that I did not need yet another one to block me off from people around me. So, I opted to just be, in each moment, in each space.

At the Dalai Lama's talk, I was standing outside, unable to hear his message for myself, and having to play crowd control to a very large group of angry people. Individuals in the crowd swore and yelled at us volunteers, tried (and some eventually succeeding) pushing past us or veering around us. How could one not be aware that you were being angry at a talk based on the concept of peace? If you did not have peace in your mind, the Dalai Lama could not give it to you. Teachers, gurus and spiritual leaders can remind you of what is ever present inside of you, but it is up to you to walk through that door.

After the exhausting talk was over, volunteers were fed a brown bag lunch. Having arrived early in the morning, standing on our feet for hours, and having tried to calm chaos, we seemed to all melt into the sidewalk, squatting with our meals.

Disappointment snuck up on me. I thought I would have been able to see the talk for myself. I had not realized that being a volunteer meant we were excluded from the event, like the people who we turned away. I had to muster a sense of appreciation for being there. People who did hear the talk would perhaps have benefited from it. I played the role I was meant to play.

Just when we were all getting ready to disperse, news came from the organizers that a short while later we would get a private visit with His Holiness. We were to report to Trump Plaza. My heart jumped for joy!

My feet ached like they hadn't in years, and it took everything I had to make it to the hotel. Sweaty, exhausted and in pain, I settled into the line the volunteers started. We were escorted into a room with chairs set up in two sections as if we were going to church, a runner leading to an elevated platform with a chair and a table with water. Select people who were not volunteers were also invited, and with their clean suits I built the assumption in my head they must have been donors to make the event happen. Index cards and pens were handed out and we were asked to write down a question for His Holiness. One of the organizers would review them, selecting several for His Holiness to respond to. I thought hard about what would I ask and what would make my question good enough to make it into the selected pile.

His Holiness arrived what seemed like an hour after we did. We were told not to touch him, take pictures, shout to him, ask him questions directly, or look at him in the eyes. It was a lot of protocol, which I assume would be minor in comparison to the instructions one would receive if meeting the Queen of England. However, people being people, those rules went out the door as he entered the room. He reached out to people. I, a few seats in from the end of the row, didn't have a chance at touching his hand like I did with Pope John Paul II when I was little.

His Holiness sat down. We sat down. He started to poke fun at himself and his glasses. The tension in the room was cut with laughter. He was a real man with a great sense of humor. He spoke to us and then answered questions from the crowd. My mind began its on and off again banter about how tired I was, how my feet ached, but it was nice to be sitting, how my question did not get picked, how I didn't get a chance to touch him. And then I realized I was silently being the angry mob. I could understand their point of view. It was natural to have emotions come and go, but ultimately it was up to me to decide how and if I acted upon them. Each one of us has free will. We can choose which emotions to feed and which ones to let go. Choosing doesn't mean we are eliminating them forever and becoming an enlightened being with no more worries in the world. Each person has their challenges. Each person holds the human emotional spectrum. In that moment, I chose to let go. I chose to listen carefully to each word he spoke, to be in the moment, and appreciate this rare opportunity given to me after a long day. I left with my heart full.

CHAPTER 11

Learning What I Liked

After the shock and disappointment of Tom, I started clubbing on weekends. I needed to go dancing. I needed time with friends. I needed to feel admired and attractive. A young woman who worked at the local PBS station I was working at, Anna, was in just the right place in her life, so we engaged in this often. My pool of friends grew and another fellow divorcee and I would hit up the dive bars other nights.

Dancing one evening, a blond haired compact man, Jonas, approached me and I was so electrified. He was my first (what I thought would have been) one-night stand. Jonas, I found out, also recently had a big break up.

We continued to talk on the phone, hang out together and go on dates. And while I had rediscovered my power as a woman, I also realized that Jonas was a Virgo. I was a Sagittarius. We had two opposite needs, desires and feelings for one another. Jonas was looking for steady. I needed some adventure.

Jonas was as sweet as could be. I felt heart-broken for him, but I could not connect with him the way he connected with me. We saw each other from time to time over the next few years, as friends, but he always then would distance himself from me because he was still feeling things for me.

A few weeks later, I met Joel at a bar in Harrisburg. After hearing more pickup lines in one sitting than ever before, I told him I was not interested. He abruptly moved away. We saw each other occasionally during the Harrisburg nightlife, but he always ignored me. On another occasion, Joel had no choice but to speak to me again as his friend and Anna were hitting it off. It looked like we were all going to be hanging out together. Better make the best of it. After a few too many drinks, Joel was at least interesting. We found common ground on music and movies. He was quite intelligent and creative. So, that evening we all went back to Joel's apartment. While Anna slipped away with her conquest, I was alone with mine.

At the end of the day, I just couldn't do it. As zen as I would like to be, I am shallow. I could not do pudge. And Joel, poor guy, was overweight. I gathered my things and without telling him the real reason I could not stay with him, I told him I needed to leave. I packed up and went for the door where Anna caught up with me asking what had happened. All I could say was, "pudge."

Phoenix

Phoenix and I met at a holistic conference one summer. This conference was for us hippies who searched for spiritual enlightenment and like-minded people.

In this one particular year, I was taking my per usual classes—Tai Chi, Qigong, Meditative Laughing with the dear Laraji, and any class I could find with the incredibly attractive John Dumas (who was lovely to look at and equally as beautiful to listen to while playing his didgeridoo). While enjoying myself and drooling over John, Phoenix and I met in Laraji's class.

Phoenix was tall with thick black hair and an olive tan. He had the scary perfect teeth and everyday he wore a tie-dye t-shirt, shorts and flip-flops.

When I first met Phoenix, he was quiet and kept to himself to the point of being rude. He sat on a cushion, meditating and refusing to speak to me—which was really unusual in a place like this. The week went on and I picked up a friend named Saṃsāra, who was a teen and as it turned out, would rather hang out with us adults, than his peers. I was happy to be around Sam who was mature beyond his years and was such fun that I would forget his age.

Phoenix started hanging out with us and a few others, slowly opening up as the days went on. Eventually, I became enamored with him. His ideas were far out there, but he was sweet. I woke up in the morning in my dorm and couldn't wait to see him. If he wasn't at breakfast I would have a momentary sigh and count the hours down until we had a class together and then lunch, free time, dinner and the lecture. In the evenings, there were always talks and after the talks more free time hanging out in the lounge listening to the sounds of Larajji and John Dumas.

His parents, also at the conference, enjoyed seeing their son be happy, and I was just as in love with them as they were with me. His parents liked to sit with us at meals until he asked them to stop so he could be with just me. Time is always so compressed at conferences, but they seem to last for years.

His Jewish parents had expanded their religious roots delving into holistic views and had been coming to the conference for years. Everyone seemed to know Phoenix and Sam (who had also grown up at the conference), so it was a wonder that I did not meet them earlier.

The three of us were like peas and carrots and corn, but Phoenix and I would sneak off to my room after we said good night as a group and talk. Or we would go hide under a tree away from everyone. On our last morning at the conference, Phoenix presented me with a rose quartz crystal heart necklace. I said I wanted to tell him something and then choked. I was still so raw from Tom, that I was afraid to put myself out there.

"Go ahead, say it. I feel the same way," Phoenix said softly.

"I love you," I responded under my breath.

"I love you, too." And we kissed again like we did so many times that week. Phoenix was a great kisser and could be quite sexy despite his abnormal tendencies to talk about ideas that had no framework in reality. I would get goose bumps with him just nearby, breathing on my neck.

Phoenix lived in a suburb of Philadelphia with his parents an hour-and-a-half away from me. We decided that after the conference was over we would try to have a relationship outside of this place.

We talked on the phone and eventually visited one another as often as possible. Making time for each other was hard, as I had a daughter to care for and he had no car. We saw each other once or twice a month and wrote to each other often and talked on the phone every day. We knew we wanted to be together forever and eventually grow our family.

Everything was peaches and cream. And then, like a single young man, he started fleeing for his life. And I like a woman looking for a mate, was blind to his flaws and held onto that bumper of a car as tightly as possible.

Let's see now, Phoenix was unemployed. Our adventures together would have to be free or I was going to pay and that was making me poor quickly. Phoenix did not have a car so it was a bus or nothing. Phoenix was a great cook and would struggle with what to make for my vegetarian picky palate, but being a trained chef, he would continue to try and feed me (as it seems like every man I had chosen to be with since my ex-husband did).

After a few months, the sex waned. Our phone conversations became less and less and he became more and more distant. He had no future goals other than "knowing" that one day he was going to "disappear."

"What do you mean by disappear?" I would ask.

"I mean one day my entire being will just cease to be here and be somewhere else."

"You're kidding, right?" I responded.

"No. I'm not going to die. I'm just going to move on. I'm working on it."

And if that wasn't enough crazy, I was crazier for asking, "Well, don't you want to be here with me instead?"

To which he would reply, "Sure, but I will go one day."

Phoenix and I had planned a picnic at Lake Redman one overcast Saturday. Much to my dismay, my brother invited himself along, rejecting my objection, and Phoenix welcomed him. This was altogether a bad idea because I had learned previously that my brother and Phoenix together was just asking for my self-esteem to plummet to the ground. Plus, the both of them were eerily similar. Neither had a desire to work, both were broke and would suck their parents dry, and both loved to point out my ever-growing list of flaws.

My brother at the time was living with Tom and Stella at the river and Phoenix loved my tribe. My brother and Phoenix would enjoy talking and being alpha males together (although Phoenix was not so much an Alpha male separated from my brother). Together, they became super critical of me, throwing judgments and comments around like there was no tomorrow. I was too uptight, worked too hard, wasn't as spiritual as them, too demanding, too judgmental, too picky, and the list went on and on.

Within a few weeks, Phoenix was making trips to see my friends at the river and my brother without even telling me he was in town. That should have been a clear red flag, but with my inability to make good decisions on men, I kept up the relationship, breathing deeply all the while.

At Lake Redman I found myself being quickly abandoned after the food was consumed. I was happy to eventually get home and quickly get rid of both men in my life. After Phoenix had left begrudgingly to go back to Philly, my brother told me to not be so upset I was the third man out at the picnic.

"I found out something you should know," my brother said. "Phoenix said his goal is to go to Brazil and sleep with lots of women."

"What???"

When Phoenix and I spoke of our future as of late, he said he would not be ready to get married until he was in his fifties. Whether I didn't push for more specifics or whether he made up reasons why, our follow up conversations seemed to revolve back to the conversation of how we couldn't have children in our fifties.

"Biology doesn't seem to want to wait that long for women, Phoenix."

"Women get pregnant all the time in their fifties."

"Uhm, no. That is why their biological clocks go crazy in their twenties because their body is saying, 'Sweetie, it's now or never.'"

He then would spout on about cases of miracles and women who do get pregnant in their fifties through modern science. I was thinking about how it was morally wrong to me to have children after the age of thirty (which side note, having a father who was almost fifty when I was born I feel gives me the right to my opinion).

But now I knew, he had his oats to sew and I was an inconvenient love in his life. Small moments of how he would argue like a child with my young daughter as to how there was no Santa should have given him away. Using sex as a means of me getting him to Central PA to see my friends should have been a sure fire clue. But love is blind.

I approached Phoenix with what he told my brother.

"You told my brother you wanted to sleep with lots of women in Brazil?"

"He told you that!" he responded angrily. "I didn't say that."

"Yes you did. Is that what you want? I thought you loved me and wanted to be with me?" I asked like an injured child.

"I can't believe I told him something in confidence and he told you."

"He's my BROTHER!"

"I didn't mean it," he argued.

"Yes you did. What do you want?" I pushed.

"I don't want to sleep with other women, but I do want to go to Brazil."

Many conversations later, it all came back to him wanting to live life and see the world and then he would settle down with me in his fifties. I was destined to be the "later" girl in his life.

I ended our relationship. My heart was already broken, but letting go was equally as hard. I used my mind and told my heart to shut up. Phoenix tried to convince me otherwise.

"Please don't worry about that now," he would say.

But how could I not worry about it now? I had my goals in life just as he had his goals in life. As silly as it sounded to some people, I was destined to be in a happy marriage. I could feel a love inside my bones I knew existed. I just needed to find it.

After a few more phone calls, Phoenix gave up. We stopped speaking, but he continued to visit my friends at the river. One time we ran into each other there and were civil to one another. He started dating someone in the area and finally had overstayed his welcome and returned home. Soon enough, I got my river and my friends back.

CHAPTER 12

Mr. Perfect 101

The world seems to present itself like a play. Just when your leading man has broken his leg and you need an understudy to take over, the universe provides. It just happened to be in my case, not an acting partner, but an Aquarius.

In 2003, at the local public media station I worked for an advertiser of ours, Flip, owned an independent movie theater, Janis Theater House. Flip was everyone's adopted father. Big build, jovial, and the biggest heart, Flip was willing to support all of the local college students. Flip loves Scotch, has a Laughing Janet from Hershey Park in his coffee house, and runs himself ragged with little sleep to run his love. He had talked with one of our sales reps about a new project he was helping with, an indie film festival.

On behalf of work, I met with Flip and his project counterpart, Mr. Perfect. Mr. Perfect—also known as Mark —Flip, a co-worker and I met for coffee at the Janis Theater House. We discussed the project and potential partnership. As someone who grew up acting, I could not refuse going to this appointment. Theresa and I went with excited blinders on to the meeting. Mark was a professor at the local college just blocks from the coffee house. He recently relocated to the area and it was his idea to start this film festival, the Onedago Film Festival, whose name came from a nearby creek.

Mark was attractive, mature, and had a smile that would light up a room. In his mid-thirties, Mark was an avid hiker, well read, loved beer, intrigued by politics, and

commitment phobic. He had a successive line of long-term
girlfriends that he was never able to commit to. And even
with a receding hairline and onset of rosacea, this
handsome man knew he had no issues with waiting.
During that meeting it was decided I would attend their
volunteer meeting within the week to find out more
information about the festival, investigate the volunteer
base and commitment of this project before it was decided
we would partner with them. The meeting was held in the
theater, which held masses of students coming to learn
what they could do to help. Mark and Flip met me in the
aisle and started talking about how to start a non-profit
association. Soon, thereafter, Mark and I started talking
via text and email, and as luck would have it, we made
plans to go hiking at my favorite spot, Peters Mountain in
Dauphin.

Peters Mountain on the Appalachian Trail was an easy
hike with paved trails and within only a few miles from the
start of this one trail, we would have access to an outhouse
and a cabin where hikers slept overnight and wrote in a
community journal. Entries included hiking experiences,
letters about themselves and sometimes poetry. I loved to
read the entries and mark my arrival with a poem.

After the awkward drive to the trail, we started on our
hike. I was glad to have beautiful distractions to create
conversation. Plus it gave me something to look at aside
from just staring at him. While we barely knew each other,
we found that we had engaging conversations, debated
about points of view, and could be quite adversarial in our
talks, which became all the more reason for me to fall head
over heels for this guy.

Being prepared for all types of weather with the
changing of the seasons and hiking in shade, I wore a t-
shirt with a sweater on top. Part way through the hike,
nervous tension and easy conversation turned into flirting.
As I changed shirts, he commented I was stripping for him
already and we only just met. Within a mile we paused at
an outlook staring across the Central Pennsylvania valley
with ladybugs crawling everywhere.

Over the next few months, I became part of the film
festival board and assisted with starting the new non-profit

organization. We were joined by a few other professors;
Stan, an employee at the theater who also had a passion
for films; and Todd, a filmmaker. The PBS station was on
board and more so, I was falling for Mr. Perfect.

In the book *Seduction* by Robert Greene, the role of the
coquette is laid out. This is apparently how one catches an
Aquarius—not my Sagittarius way of chasing, attacking
and devouring. As my best friend Arabella and I talked over
the next few months, she kept advising me on how to play
the role, and while I completely fell short of even
attempting this, he was completely unconsciously
successful in playing the role.

When I met Mark, my instincts were to chase this man
down and make him mine. While at first it was pure
attraction, it soon became love for me. I loved a man who
became my very good friend. We would talk on the phone
for hours, email and text for days at a time, and suddenly
he would disappear not returning any communication only
to making me want more. We would go out to dinner or for
beer and he would always pay unless my masculine side
kicked in and insisted to pay for the both of us. And we
didn't always go to the nearest bar or a crappy restaurant.
Two vegetarians who loved food, we would head out to nice
and sometimes romantic restaurants, leaving me always
wondering if we were finally on a date.

His strong views on education matched mine and
nothing would motivate me more to go back to school than
that of a man I needed to woo. So, I enrolled in Harrisburg
Area Community College, transferred as many credits as
they would take and started going to school part time.
Fortunately for me, I had a wonderful boss, Henry, who
was pursuing his Master's Degree and would let me take
an extended lunch break twice a week for one of my
classes. I squeezed other ones in during evenings and
weekends. Suddenly I was knee deep in homework and
school loans, but enjoying every minute of it.

While that whole eating thing was convenient for both
of us being vegetarian, he loved spicy foods, so naturally I
did too. I ate spicy foods, and often. I hated spicy foods. I
could not even stand table pepper. However, when those
Cajun fries came out, I ate them. Out to dinner and a

jalapeño on my salad? I ate it. And not only did I eat it, but I proceeded not to drink water afterwards to prove I could indeed withstand spicy foods. Oh my God, the horror of spicy foods!

Not to mention my issue with jam. Fruit is fruit and should be eaten whole or juiced. Squish it and it's just not fruit anymore. Maybe it's a texture thing for me. However, ask me what was for breakfast at his house? Bread and jam, which I ate without a complaint.

We were outwardly affectionate towards each other in private—hugging, cuddling, and giving each other back massages and foot rubs. In person, we stood an arm's length apart, eyes always connecting and words aimed towards each other's ears. I think some of his friends thought we were dating when we went out together, but he only ever introduced me as his friend.

Not all of our engagements were flirting, but were full of debates about politics, historical figures, authors and books, and life in general. He was someone I could call to talk about my day and complain about the human race. The subject of my daughter though was always kept on the back burner, protected. In fact, we had known each other for more than half a year before I had him meet my daughter at a dinner party I was having.

Dinner parties for me were an exciting time to have good friends come over, dim the lights, light candles, cook an exquisite meal and engage in stimulating conversation. On this one particular evening I had invited Mark, my friend Todd, a few other friends and my best friend and soul sister, Arabella, from Florida (to meet Mark of course).

Now at this time, Todd the filmmaker had also peeked my interest greatly. Todd a tall lean blond haired man was one of the kindest most humble people I had met in a long time. He and Mark were complete opposite ends of the spectrum, only meeting in the middle in terms of age. Both in their thirties, Mark was secure in his profession, boisterous, great sense of humor, brown hair, and flirtatious. Todd was quiet and almost shy, was the person to laugh at jokes more than make them, would always be courteous with women not because he was supposed to for appearance, but would hold a door because he genuinely wanted to take care of you. My infatuation with Todd happened during the first Onedago Film Festival board meeting I attended, but with no hope for anything with Todd, that became a thought in the back of my mind. But then poor Todd unknowingly would win me over with his charm, and then reverse direction asking me for girl advice with catching my friend, CJ's heart.

Arabella, also being an eloquent conversationalist, dived into the wine and the topics. My daughter was sent to bed early so we adults could enjoy our evening. After dinner that evening, Arabella who wound up having a drunken heated conversation with Mark about commitment issues men have (aka why don't you date Susan here), she then helped me clean up and told me Todd was nice, but Mark was a pain in the ass Aquarius who did not want to be caught.

Mark had left with a rather bad taste in his mouth from Arabella who was pursuant in her quest to understand men. Needless to say, he was a gentleman and did not insult my friend, but certainly was happy she did not live close by. Within a few weeks, we were back to our same routine of push pull, talking and not talking. He started making comments about not wanting to do anything to disturb our friendship. I would text him to look up at the moon one evening, he would say how beautiful it was and then off the planet he was for a few days visiting Saturn or the Moon or just grading papers.

Arabella would say to me, "If anyone could go from friendship to sex, it would be an Aquarius. And if anyone could round them up and lead them that way, it would be you, Susan."

Way to go me. And it only took eight months. Eight months of trying every natural and written seduction method known to woman and all I needed was an evening of too much wine that disabled me from driving home and watching movies.

Mr. Perfect was even perfect in bed. I truly did not know that I was having bad sex my whole life until I experienced him. I mean, what the hell was I doing with my time?

Way to go for the nerd who watched a lot of porn and read "Kama Sutra?" Frankly the entire thought of going back to sampling other men frightened me. Talking with girlfriends one day, I firmly established that most men were a) selfish in bed, and b) had no skills.

Aside from the good sex, it all went downhill from there. "You realize this will eventually end," and the "I thought we were only booty call friends," and we can't forget the "I'm here to service you when you need to be serviced," were some of the many ways one might see that he was a prick. But alas, I was enjoying the attention, the sex, and the friendship. I thought the occasional dinner, drinks or breakfast created the date scenario. No, no. This is when we start to realize that Mr. Perfect is really not perfect. Who would have thought?

My pattern, if I was not blind enough to see it at this time, was that I so desperately wanted to find and be with love that I would change anything about myself to make me fit the picture of their perfect woman. Even though I am rebellious by nature, I would follow stupid man rules. Kevin wanted blond, short hair. After much pleading, what did I do? Dye my hair blond and eventually cut it. Needless to say, I looked awful. Phoenix refused to have me listen to the radio around him because the energy waves were negative and of course, I did all of the paying for everything. Mr. Perfect wanted it all with no obligations, so I let him have it.

I had a dream one night that we were married and living in a house with lots of doors. There was a staircase with a wooden banister and the house was quiet despite the children. I had them in a room with a closed door while he was in another room with the door closed. I tried to get him to be with us, but he was too busy. I knew this would be our life together, but still I pursued it.

During Oktoberfest at ABC bar in Harrisburg, one of his friends asked how his evening out with a young woman went. They had gone to the movies, a note to which he never mentioned and actually lied about when we talked earlier in the week. He tried to avoid the question and when his friend pressed talking about "the date," Mark kept correcting saying it wasn't a date. After a few days, I could not hold it in anymore and told him it bothered me even though we were not dating and if he was going to screw around, I needed to know for my own physical safety. He denied the date, saying it was a friend and he was not dating anyone or sleeping with anyone since we started our "friends with benefits" deal.

One day he had a dinner party in honor of Robert Burns full of haggis and poetry with his college professor buddies, where I was once again introduced as his friend. Like the movie *He's Not That Into You*, I was there to help fill the food bowls, clean up, wash dishes, and get what people needed, but as a friend. I saw one female professor in particular look at me with a look of curiosity. What did she think? "Why is this young girl so stupid to put up with being called a friend?" "Are they involved?" But I was focused on him. I watched him watch me in this room of PhDs with me having no college degree and holding my own. As impressed as he may have been with me, as much as his friends and co-workers may have loved me, I could never achieve his standards. Appearance was everything to him, but being an Aquarius, he would never admit it—or perhaps he too was so unaware of his own psychosis. Aquarius men play the coquette with utter perfection. Hot and cold, keeping you always slightly off balance wondering what is happening. They will always say their motivation is for the greater good of the world, but when it boils down to it, really it's only their image. Their image is everything. And I being a single mother, with crooked teeth, a broken family, and my hippie ways, was not the ideal woman to bring home to mom.

For his birthday, I threw him a surprise party on a Friday evening with his close professor pals at a local pub he frequented near his apartment. Complete with cake and beer candles and me calling myself his friend in front of his friends. Back at his apartment many pitchers of beer later, he seemed to profess that he had feelings for me. And what do I do? What should a drunken woman in a precarious relationship never do? You guessed it. "I love you," slipped from my lips.

After that party, things went downhill. We talked little that week only to talk about our day and how much he despises parties and attention. One week after his party, he came to my house. For the sake of my ego, the evening shall be called "the breakup." Although by now the mass delusion of love had completely blinded me from the inevitable—we were never an item. Who knew that sex with friends could not constitute for more, what with all of those steady invitations, phone calls and insinuating emails? I was blind. I had not known how to date yet.

Alcohol helps heal wounds, impending doom, and mask nervousness, if only for a little while. With this in mind, I started out the night in question with a glass of red wine in order to anesthetize myself for the future encounter—I thought he was going to pronounce his undying love for me. I then proceeded to hide my daughter from any clocks so the sheer fact that it was 7:30 P.M. would be disguised as her 8:00 P.M. bedtime.

Post bedtime I ran around the house putting those final touches I was known for—incense burning, candles lit, jazz music in the background, and oh that wine.

Upon his arrival, I made sure the bottle of wine was safely in grabbing distance. Meanwhile I savored my glass and started an uneventful conversation.

"So, how was work today?"

After talking nonsense for about two hours, I realized as I leaned to kiss his lips and he turned his head for me to catch his cheek, something was wrong.

"What did I say to you Friday night?" he asked. And suddenly I knew I was not about to hear how I was future Mrs. Perfect. Suddenly from his mouth come words of "friendship" and how all sexual encounters from this moment further are to end. He never wanted anything to interfere with our friendship.

"I want to know where you are fifteen years from now, not wonder where you are," he said.

"Duh! You could know where I am fifteen years from now by being with me," I thought to myself. Apparently education does not equal common sense or overcoming the "screw 'em and leave 'em" attitude of men.

After Phoenix, I decided that showing my emotions in front of men did not suit any situation. So, I grabbed the bottle of wine and drank heavily. In an effort to smooth things out while he yakked on about God knows what, I decided it was a smart thing to get out the Susan photo album full of cute pictures of me as a kid. Why? Well of course that would really entice him to love me after all! Truly I wanted to kick him out of my house and my life that very moment, but my manners prevented me from doing so. So, I did what I did best, punished myself.

After about another hour of sheer torture, he left. I immediately called Arabella because I love her; she knew that he was coming over and seriously, how many people do I know that stay up that late?

Arabella and I decided Mark was an Eternal Bachelor. These are men who will never get married. Do not be fooled. Only at the inclination that marriage seems like a good decision suddenly (usually when they have reached their mid-life crisis and see death knocking at the door). When the decision is made, all ex-girlfriends will realize it has nothing to do with the woman he selected. It has to do with the decision in his mind and the closest thing that is identifiable as a woman.

Emergency call with Arabella turned into drunken chain-smoking fest on porch proceeded by crying myself to sleep while dreaming of Mr. Perfect with our once perfect life in the perfect future. And then I woke up.

My heart was broken. He left and the mess he left had to go to bed to start her day as a broken single mother who had to take care of a kid and work despite her emotions.

A divorced woman who is looking for a new life has seen the show. She knows the games, she knows motivations, she sees the truth and yet she ignores it like a blind person with no senses whatsoever. The dream is set and she is looking for the Ken doll to insert into place, regardless of whether he fits the scene or not. It's the dream that drives her: the dream of a better life. The dream she envisioned when she was a little girl playing dolls. The dream she had in high school imagining her wedding day. Even a broken marriage cannot kill that dream. If anything, pursuing it becomes stronger.

I spent a year of my life trying to contort myself into his idea of a perfect world and in the end, was too ignorant to see it wouldn't be worth it. My life was now tied to reading massive amounts of boring textbooks, writing papers and being in debt. Without sex. Dumb. Dumb.

A few months later Todd had a fabulous party at his home in Mt. Gretna. The community was a walking one so you parked your car on the street and walked through little sidewalks up to houses. Ted drew cute sayings on the ground like, "Saunter this way," as he guided friends, neighbors, and artists to his house. Once there, he taped a picture of a famous person on your back you so that you had to meet people. You were limited to asking three questions to each person about the picture. I was quite impressed with Todd's way of getting approximately fifty artists to network and meet one another. I knew few people there and mingled as much as a natural hermit can. And then suddenly within an hour, Mark was there with a meaty blond. We avoided each other the entire evening, as I purposefully tried to become the center of people's conversation groups and talked with Todd about the awkward relationship Mark and I just shared. Todd being Todd had no idea.

While waiting for the bathroom (girls always have lines!), Mark's date was in line. She was drunk and could barely stand up. "Aren't you Mark's ex-girlfriend?" she asked. And while I knew she meant no harm in asking, I had no desire to talk with her and luckily the bathroom door just opened. So, now after a year of friendship, of being used for the good of humanity, I was an ex-girlfriend. I wonder if this is how all of his former lovers felt. He would tell me how he was a still friend with almost all his exes. I wonder if they too only knew they were once a couple after the entire disaster was over, and from someone else.

Todd and I began to hang out and talk more. He was comforting. And while I continued to always be attracted to Todd, I felt way too damaged to ever try anything. It probably helped that almost every conversation he asked for girl advice. One night we went to a movie and he paid. I paid for our concessions because in my mind I was trying to figure out if this was a date or not. I could not go through the unknowing again and my paying for concessions was my way of putting my stamp on this evening as this is not a date unless you say the word date. He looked really confused by my paying for popcorn and drinks. After the movie he asked me to go with him for

Chinese food. We had a great dinner with me wondering what this was. Was this me and my incredibly wonderful friend Todd? Or was this Todd not asking me but taking me on a date. That was the last time we spent time together alone. The next time Todd and I saw each other was a year later on his film set where I did body shots for him. We barely spoke. And soon thereafter he was off to LA making dreams come true.

In the end, I realized that while Mr. Perfect truly was hopelessly flawed, I moved towards perfecting myself because of him. And thus, he still deserves his title.

CHAPTER 13

Single, Spiritual and Looking for Love

One day I was reading *Shamballa Sun*, a magazine that focuses on meditation and Buddhism. There was an ad for a spiritual singles online dating service. My first thought was, *"Yes. If I was ever going to do one, that's the one."* My second thought was, *"Heck no. I want subtle spiritual men, not someone who will use it as a crutch to block engaging in the sometimes ugly components of relationships."*

I thought of how my ad would read. "Single woman. Loves outdoors, children, pets, and the arts. Does yoga, meditation. Speaks to dead people. Looking for male with a great body, who has mutual interests, not afraid of commitment and has oodles of patience. Will eat dessert first, read middle of books last. Can roll with the punches of life and forgives easily and quickly. Oh and is not someone looking to mate with other women and not a sociopath."

I think that would be it. But our needs are always evolving, are they not?

My best friend, Arabella, told me one day, "You are a restless soul," which is a polite way of perhaps saying that I might have ADD. My entire life has been movement—either literally or figuratively. My childhood was shaped by it.

I felt like the eternal child of everyone I encountered. And everyone had advice for me. Why not, right? Soap operas are not this exciting.

He's a jerk. He's nice. You shouldn't be dating anyone, but embracing your freedom and concentrating on your daughter. You don't need a man. Why would you even want a man? You need to date more because we need entertainment since you're the only single person left in the office. Trust me, I've been there. Learn from my mistakes.

Learn from my mistake. Learn from my mistakes. That was a famous line. Almost as much as, "When I was in your shoes."

Perhaps advice came from those who thought they could mold and shape me into what they wanted or missed out on. Perhaps they were trying to spare me from the pain they once endured. But I'll tell you what, as a mother, I believed in letting your child grow wings and learn to fly. No child will adhere to the advice of their elders as they mature because life is to be experienced. And one cannot experience through the cautious words of another.

One day, when my friend Missy and I were chatting, she could hear something in my voice. Someone heard my war cry!

"Would you like it if I did not tell you what to do anymore?" she asked.

"Yes. Thanks. I just want someone to listen," I replied. Listen, help me have the strength to move on and analyze the hell out of the new muse in my life. That's all. It's not easy being the epitome of scrutiny all of the time. Or at least that's how it felt. I wanted a shoulder to lean on while I learned and grew from a painful experience. I wanted someone to help me figure out why men really were from Mars and how in the world we could even be in the same species.

After two years of putting my private daily life at the mercy of those around me, I learned that the opinion of those around me is not what I wanted. I decided to keep everything inside and listen to my own inner voice. My soul knew what the answers were all of the time anyway. All I wanted was someone to listen every now and then. I quickly found out though that everyone has an opinion they wanted to share. Everyone was subjective. Some were pessimistic: others, too positive. I didn't want that anymore. I wanted privacy.

CHAPTER 14

The Valentine's Day Massacre

I went as a rebel in disguise after the let down of Mr. Perfect and headed out to two wild nights successively. Night one—The Bachelorette Party. Filled with tons of bisexual ladies sending off the future Mrs. Anna Bass into her future of wedlock. One of Mark's co-workers started speaking with me a few weeks after Mark and I stopped talking. Mark commented while we were friends that his friend, fan of Pigmys, liked me. I think he was a history professor.

I invite the Pigmy fan to join us for when the men were meeting the ladies later (as the Bachelor wanted to make sure his prize is safe and behaving herself). After many whiskeys on his part and many Captain and Cokes on mine, we spent the evening dancing together, watching me kiss my good friend CJ, driving drunken girls home, had many kisses and a short teasing massage. The following day after many tears were once again shed over Mr. Perfect, my brother whisked me away to the local bar where apparently to my lack of observation, the men were swarming like a pack of bees ready to sting. According to one bar patron, after my brother's announcement that I was his sister, there is was a collective sigh and silence in the room, quickly followed by a healthy competition for my attention. Corey and Eric decide to steal me away for a couple of hours for dancing and roaming the town of York. While Corey's goal was for everyone to have fun, it became clear that he had other intentions, as the only time I could be by myself was if I was dancing on the bar.

While traveling from the Hardware Bar to Cobblestones, Eric mentioned Jazz, and it was all over from there. We spend the entire evening talking about common interests while he spouts, "Oh, my God. You are stealing my heart." Due to my new celibacy rule where I followed the Buddhist philosophy of no sex without love and commitment, we spent the after-hours cuddling and talking (not that he didn't try to no end to get me in bed with him, he even got completely naked hoping something would happen).

Eric, while not on my list of stable partnerships, seemed to still be a very nice man. He pursued me, calling every other day, and we met for lunch about a week after we met. Following lunch, I had booked a date for Valentine's Day, as well as a date for the following Saturday.

When Valentine's Day arrived, it turned out to be the biggest bust, beginning with Eric leaving me a message confirming our date. Next, spending hours getting ready and waiting around for him. And finally him not showing up, but then calling and inviting me to hang out at his friend's house. What made the evening worse was agreeing to go out with my brother to forget the disaster of an evening, only to have my brother run a tab, which he couldn't pay, and ended up with me driving around to find an ATM at 1 A.M. to pay it off.

By now I was disgusted with men, and my following of *ahimsa* (a yogic philosophy of do no harm) was being challenged. I read an article that said a man can fall in love with a woman instantly based on whether he would sleep with her or not. We have this clash of goals in our little bizarre species. Men are programmed biologically to keep the species populated while women are programmed to keep the species alive. He looks for fertility. She looks for protection. So, when does biology for men take a back seat and turn into committed bliss?

It seemed to me like it didn't matter how much time you invest in a man. He's ready when he is. If you've spent five years with a man who is not ready, watch out. Two women later, he's ready and it makes no difference who she is because now he's made up his mind. How many women friends of mine have said, "I'm so tired of raising a man?" Or, "He just met her and now they're getting married. I was with him for two years!"

After Eric, I continued to wander, and be wooed, and be heart broken. I had a forty-five year old admirer I had no attraction to, whom I met during a play. I had a fifty-year-old Republican who didn't call back after I refused having sex with him. This man was certainly from the "Catch and Release Program," as Arabella and I call it. Men who you know have been in a long-term relationship or marriage. (A week-long relationship or a six-month marriage does not constitute for this term.) They have been released back into society without any labeling as to whether they have been rehabilitated or not. After that I had random dates, random bar calls, and a randomly lonely heart.

CHAPTER 15

It Gets Worse?

In one of my adventures out with my friend Sherri, we went to Flapjack's: a dive bar where she could see her friends. I met a red neck; at this point, I thought I needed to open my mind and see if the case truly was a male breed issue, regardless of education, money and upbringing. He happened to be someone who Sherri knew and commented how she thought he was a nice guy. So, nice guy and I hung out and danced to jukebox music. We all headed back to his house, which was beautiful and grown up. I stood my ground that we would not go anywhere physically. He never called after that night.

A few weeks later, I was at a bar hearing jazz music. The saxophone player wearing a suit and a fedora bought me a drink. We had a great time talking about music, film and art. We headed back to his house for the night. The next morning, he looked at me like he made the biggest mistake of his life. I immediately knew in my gut he had a girlfriend. I rounded myself up and told him I'd talk to him later. I knew he would never call, which he didn't.

After that I met a young guy in his early twenties with light blond hair, the bluest of eyes, who had an interest in spirituality. We spent many evenings together going for drinks, watching movies, and talking. After a few weeks it appeared he was more interested in being friends than in a relationship. After an evening of frank conversations about what was going on with us, neither of us called each other again.

At the river, someone mentioned how they recently had a year of silence on a retreat. I coupled this with a recent article I read on keeping thoughts to yourself so you are sharing with yourself. I made a more concerted effort to go out to dinner myself and to the movies. When I had joys, I shared my joys with myself. When I had sadness, I talked myself through them. If I heard a funny joke, I repeated it to myself. I became my own entertainment. I was learning to be all I needed. I knew I was stubborn, blind, and hopelessly flawed, but aren't we all are broken birds trying to put ourselves back together?

I started changing what I needed and wanted. I appreciated myself more. I enjoyed my own company. I didn't need anyone to fix me or fill something missing inside of me.

I decided to learn from my disaster succession of men. One day, I took a scrap piece of paper and started writing down all of the positive qualities I was looking for in a partner. I folded it up and kept it in my purse. I had started this after Mr. Perfect and continued until every piece of white space was covered. I was learning about (and reminding myself) of what I needed, what was non-negotiable, in a relationship. I reminded myself even psychics could be blind in the search for love. But I didn't want to be blind anymore. Instead, I wanted to be whole in every way possible.

CHAPTER 16

She Will Be Loved

A two-year process I put more time, money and love into than any other project before was the next day—The Onedago Film Festival. My mind was in a frenzy of anxiety, worrying if everything was prepared and if the audience would come. While driving home from work, a vision pushed through the distraction. I saw a man with blond hair, facial stubble and wearing what I thought to be a brown cowboy hat. I called Arabella telling her about my vision and how I think this was going to be a future love of mine. Little did I know in my quick manifesting world, was he to enter my life in the next twenty-four hours.

Everyone was checking in with me in the Friday madness of the film festival: the volunteers, random audience members, the board and the filmmakers. Suddenly, a blond-haired man sporting facial stubble and a brown, patterned hat walks down the hall towards me and introduces himself. In my moment of frenzy and confusion I ask for the pronunciation of his last name and that of the other filmmaker who was not present. "Kiss Kiss," I spelled out based on the sound. And he departed and I kept the momentum of the evening going.

For the rest of the weekend my mind scattered amongst the festival. However, we had several opportunities to chat. Charlie tagged along with board members and filmmakers alike to local bars after the festival. On Friday evening, sitting on wooden bar stools at a cocktail table, I could not shake the feeling I had with Charlie.

On Saturday evening, huddled into a small room with a large group of filmmakers and volunteers, I decided to see if he could handle my other worldly side.

"Are you easily weirded out?" I asked him.

"No," Charlie replied.

"No, seriously. Are you easily weirded out because I have something very bizarre to share with you."

"No, go ahead," he answered.

And I told him of my vision two days before.

"Well, when I saw you I felt this odd connection to you which caught me by surprise. If you didn't notice, I got the hell right out of there because I didn't know what that was about," he said back surprisingly.

After the bar, three of us went back to Charlie's motel room. Hanging out in the bathroom was a Martian toothbrush. Who was this guy? Was I falling for a weird Canadian stalker?

I stayed a bit after everyone left. We chatted more staring into each others eyes propped up on elbows on the dirty motel carpet. After a bit longer, I was too drunk to drive home and he invited me to spend the night. As we lay innocently in his bed, he asked, "May I kiss you?"

After the festival was over, I emailed him saying that because of the connection I felt, I wanted to talk more. He said he was debating emailing me the same thing. So, we started chatting on the phone.

A month later I got a ride to Niagara Falls, New York with my friend Anna. She was visiting her family for Thanksgiving and my daughter was with her father and family for the weekend. Charlie and I made arrangements to meet at a Blues/Jazz Bar on the U.S. side first, followed by my first trip to Canada.

With the sun having set, Niagara Falls looked like a ghost town with storefront after storefront closed for business. It looked like the economy had taken a serious beating here. Anna dropped me off and with a small travel bag in hand, and I entered a dimly lit blues bar.

I peeked my head around to see if I could even recognize him. Moments later the very tall 6'5 Charlie, came over to me, kissed me on the cheek and brought me over to the table. It was awkward! I didn't know this man.

We spoke on the phone and emailed, but this was in person. It was so odd. How do I make conversation now? I was stuck here while Anna was in Buffalo for a few days, so I had to give it a go.

Within an hour, we drove over the Rainbow Bridge into Canada in his gold Saturn. We stopped on the Canada Niagara side. Not knowing I was not a fan of anything scary, Charlie took me into a haunted house where I told him I was chicken and never did these things. I then closed my eyes for most of the tour, snuggled into his side, while he put his arm around me and guided me through as quickly as possible.

He apologized and thought it would be romantic to be scared together. Charlie was a huge fan of horror films. He thought that as I got scared I would cuddle into him. Which I did, but panicked the entire time.

We walked over to the falls, watching the multi-colored light show on the water pouring down. The sound of water always soothed me. We spent a bit of time out in the cold just watching each other, occasionally admiring the force of man and nature. When I could take the chill of the evening no more, he drove me to his house in Toronto.

Charlie rented a house with roommates who were all invisible that evening. He lived in a loft-like room with no door on the third floor. His room was full of posters, a bed on the floor, a couch, and a mess. Typical bachelor. After the first initial awkwardness, we spent the next couple of days sight-seeing and me learning about him and Toronto. He is a proud Canadian citizen!

How much stock do you put into a relationship where the other person is eight hours, a country and a lifestyle away from your own? Do you love for the sake of love in spite of the inevitable hurt that is bound to come?

"It's like a Greek tragedy," he told me once. "Where you know the main character will have a sword drawn through his body and it all will end. But despite all of these elements working against us, I want to try to make it work."

Two people—both trying not to love, trying not to mentally acknowledge that one or both will wind up firmly in pain in the end. We were two people trying not to let go of one another, all the same.

Meanwhile, Mr. Perfect called me driving home one evening. Men have a sixth sense to know when a woman is seriously taken. Mark and I had not spoken in weeks.

"I'm not ready to let you go," he said. My ears were open. My heart jumped. I would have done anything for this man.

After moving around the subject and not knowing how to express himself, Mark finally acknowledged what I needed and then said, "How about if you are not married by the time you are thirty and I am not married by the time I am forty, we'll marry each other."

"Are you asking me to hang up on you?" I could not believe what he was saying. What kind of commitment was this? It was a man who could not make one and afraid of trying to. This was all he could give me.

"It's not good enough," I said, ending our conversation.

What was the point of love if we look at it from a practical standpoint? At the end of the day, shouldn't love be so rare that we dive into the deep unknown waters to see what it's like? Shouldn't we move mountains for it? Love is a crazy adventure where you jump knowing your parachute may not open. If we stay true to our minds and ignore our heart, how are we really actively engaging in love? Love isn't safe. Love isn't something to observe.

I was so tired of chasing after a guy. I was so tired of trying for both people. Yes, the obvious thought here is if he wasn't participating, there were never two of you to begin with.

I'm a sci-fi, comic book reading geek and I love *Star Trek: The Next Generation*. In one episode, *Lessons*, Picard finds love with crewmember, Nella. This episode is heartbreaking. Picard falls in love. Nella is sent to do a dangerous job. He is heartbroken thinking she may have died. But in the end, she lives and everyone's happy. What's heartbreaking to me is that it would have been better if she died. In the end, he could not give up his career, his life, to form a relationship with her. His mind chose. His heart was quieted. What was so much more important than taking that risk of love?

What was so hard about saying I love you and then going for it? When I love you, I love you. I may be scared to go deep with all of the emotional baggage at the get go, but I will brave your reaction and tell you. I will show you through small acts of kindness.

CHAPTER 17

Love Ya

It's a never-ending conversation you have with yourself in your mind. Who should say, "I love you," first? I like going first because I want to share my feelings (plus I just like taking charge—that Sagittarius archer). However, the human side of me cowers in fear of rejection and so called lunacy in the name of announcing it too early on.

I fell in love with Charlie the second day I knew him. I could pinpoint the moment I knew I loved him. I lay there in his arms in his motel room, suddenly overwhelmed with emotion. I was frustrated that I could feel that way with someone who lived eight hours away. In the dark that night, I whispered in silence, "I love you." He didn't hear me. He wasn't meant to.

Who in their right mind would ever actually have made that utterance out loud? I don't think there would have even been a hello the next morning. Simply, a "Hey, uhm, see you later at the reception," as he slyly dashed out of town.

By the new year, I started to get the weird telephone ending. I would laugh telling him I could not help it because his voice would change at the end of a call to a soft, yet serious, "Good night," as he lingered on the phone for a few extra moments.

A little while later, the endings started to change to "I, uh... I uh..." at which point my inclination was that he was going to say the "L" word. I freaked out. It's one thing to love someone, but it is definitely another thing to hear it when you are not ready.

Luckily the words never exited his mouth and I read somewhere that Capricorns take forever to utter them and then when they do, it will be the last time you ever hear it again. The end. I felt comforted.

When I visited in November, Charlie told me, "I can't separate love from sex." So, I asked myself, "Self, does this mean that he loves you?" It was way too soon to tell. Besides, we attempted to consummate our relationship three times that weekend.

On the way home with Anna a few days later, my mind wandered back to his previous statement. If he could not separate love from sex, did that mean he loved me now because we sort of slept together or did it mean he did not love me because of our failed sexual experience? Perhaps he felt pushed into sex by me or his body, but his heart was not ready and then the whole thing was a flop.

Would that statement be considered a non-evasive way of proclaiming ones love without actually having to say, "I love you?" After all, he would have freaked me out. It had only been a month. I was the silent psycho. The world could not handle two at once at this point in time.

After the visit, his typical email sign off "Good Speed Always" (apparently an airline slogan that he found most amusing) was followed by "with love." Upon first seeing that phrase, I quickly called Anna over to read the email.

"Anna... Anna... Anna, you need to come over here. Like now. Like right now and see this."

As she approached my cubicle, I felt like I couldn't breathe, my heart sunk into the deep reaches outside my body and I was going to throw up. Could anyone say commitment-phobic?

"What does this mean?" I asked as I pointed to the computer screen. "Does this mean he loves me?"

"Gosh no. He's just a nice guy saying more nice-guy things," she replied at which point I became the typical fiery girl. Now that I had it in my head he loved me, no one could take that away from me. So, as I made my case for the next five minutes following her back to her cubicle, I realized that he did love me. I'd known this all along. I didn't need to be swayed by the uninformed opinions of others or prove anything to them, either. Ha!

And then I did it. One month and sixteen days after we met, I prepared an email to say how I felt.

"Hope you had a wonderful Britney Spears day! Love ya, Susan."

(Side note: Britney Spears was a joke as he was having a mental breakdown after midnight one evening trying to figure out how Britney Spears could have a Double CD greatest hits album when she only ever put out three CDs.)

"Love ya." Was I signing this relationships death warrant? Was I about to flush everything down the toilet? Perhaps since he gave me a scare with the "with love" he deserved it right back.

I knew what I was doing. I signed it off with a "Love ya" because that's how I felt. I felt like my email was casual relaxed. I always said, "Love ya" to Arabella. I had many friends, male and female, with whom I say, "Love ya" or "I love you" with. Why couldn't I do it now?

"Because you are dating him... and it is too soon. Whatever happened to guarding your heart? You obviously cannot guard your heart if you're allowing yourself to love him," lectured Anna, which just made me mad all over again.

I tinkered with endings to my email and then let it sit there for five hours while I pondered over how he would react. Would he just think, "Aww. That's cute." Would he have an anxiety similar to mine? Would he not even pay attention to it?

I quick emailed Sherri. Of course she said to do it. So, naturally I played devil's advocate as to why I should not.

And then I got real angry with Anna for always bringing me down to earth or being pessimistic about the positive light of my love life. Finally, I decided to ignore everyone and be me. I hit the send button and it was off.

In December I visited him again for New Year's eve, asking a homeless guy to ring his doorbell for me. Charlie didn't know I was coming for a visit. I wanted to surprise him. Carrying with me a three-foot tall Christmas stocking, I finally showed myself when he was confused by the man at the door. A month later, he said, "I love you" on the phone. The same day, I received one of his letters (we were also writing letters back and forth via snail mail) that said he loved me. I said it back, too.

CHAPTER 18

Charlie had the qualities I needed in a relationship—patience, the ability to provide stability without suffocation, and he adored me and my daughter.

As a single mother, I was not messing around. By November, I was telling him my long-term goals were to get married and have more children. I had seen the show (over and over again), and was not in the mood to see anymore. I was sincere with what I needed and Charlie was a good man who loved me and wanted the same things I wanted. I was a woman on a mission with a timeline.

I am an avid reader. I can devour three to four books a week. I go through my phases of reading like a mad person until after several months' time when I need a break from reading altogether. Aside from my insatiable need to read a multitude of books, I read the first chapter first, the last chapter next and then the middle. I have to know the ending. If the ending is disappointing, there is no need for me to put myself through the emotional torture of bonding to characters that get screwed in the end. Movies and books to me are my own personal adventures. I become the characters. I live their lives. I'm in no mood for struggle without a happy ending.

And so it is with relationships. I need to know the ending so I can enjoy the book. It's the illusion of security that keeps me going. Without knowing someone loves me and shares the same goals as me, it just really seems like a waste of time. Why do I want to love you if you are going to tell me a few months into a relationship it was all for fun? I can have fun at the mall without having my ego blown to smithereens.

He included me in his daily life, if even from afar. He came to visit or we met halfway in Ithaca whenever we could. In Ithaca, we rented a yurt from a gentleman and his wife we discovered when looking for lodging. The open land had this magnificent round yurt with a folding couch, large center rug and fireplace. We had to go outside to use the outhouse, but the evenings were spent snuggling in this amazing space. During the day, we hunted through bookstores, ate meals at Moosewood Restaurant, and went to the local farmer's market.

Charlie accepted everything there was about me: my need for adventure, change, silliness, and my need to read the last chapter of a book before I started it. When I was diagnosed with HPV after two biopsies came back positive for pre-cancer cells, I called him crying. That evening, in the dark of winter, he drove all day and night in the snow to sit with me. He put off work to be with me after cryo surgery. By May, we were engaged.

Sitting in my car after attending the annual "Artsfest," a weekend long festival filled with art, food and film in downtown Harrisburg, Charlie proposed.

"I don't have a dog or a ring, but I know I want to be with you for the rest of my life. Will you marry me?"

In August we arranged to drive to Boston to get married. I wanted our wedding to be just us. I've never been one for pomp and circumstance and saying your "I Dos" in front of a hundred people wasn't a way I wanted to express my deepest feelings. I had done that with Kevin, and never felt comfortable.

I made arrangements with the state of Massachusetts for my friend Karen to marry us. Karen had moved to Boston within the past year. She was the ultimate choice for me as she had been someone who was so special in my life. I never visited Massachusetts before, having only heard stories from my mother about how lovely it was. I'm not sure what drew me to Massachusetts. Charlie was up for it as he had never visited it and he loved history.

Upon arrival in Boston, we went to the courthouse before they closed for the weekend to fill out an application, got settled into Karen's small apartment and started hunting for locations to get married. Karen was so kind that she had put up a curtain in her living room for us to stay while pulling a mattress into the kitchen for her.

She lived in such a quaint part of Boston with so many historic, beautiful homes. In the evenings, Charlie and I walked around enjoying the area. During the day, we looked at parks in Boston, beaches in Gloucester, finally settling on a beach in Salem. The rocky beach was covered in green moss and was once home to a fort. Charlie and I had our personal reflections of style: History for him, nature for me.

The next day, Karen, Charlie and I loaded into her car for the beach. The tide had come in taking our exact spot away, but being the young lovers we were, we didn't care. Karen said a few words. Charlie and I spoke our personal written vows to one another. As I was accepting this man to be my husband, my feet ran as cold as they could get. I was here. I was committed. I loved this man. Was I making a mistake? Was he not as perfect as I could possibly get? Of course there was the issue with him still living part-time in Toronto where his work was. Our married life would be like our dating life—commuting and seeing each other every few weeks. But we were capturing love at full force. We were love pioneers—not afraid to take the dangerous road ahead. Pecking at the back of my mind was that if I changed my mind over the course of the weekend, I would not have to file the marriage certificate on Monday.

Charlie wore a simple blue shirt and pants while I wore a white cotton dress I picked up at a beach-like shop when we were last in Ithaca. I bucked up and focused back on the task at hand, an earthquake shaking my entire insides under the weight of what I was doing. When we were done, we posed for pictures and decided to celebrate with dinner at a local Indian restaurant.

The next day my nerves were far more calm. It also didn't hurt that Karen, Charlie and I went to see a talk with Buddhist monk, Thich Nhat Hahn at Boston University. The three of us sat for hours listening to the wise monk on his tour of peace. The rest of our time in Massachusetts was spent in Salem taking in the historic place, inspiring an idea for a story waiting to be written, and being the geeky versions of ourselves, eating pizza and watching *Star Trek: The Next Generation*.

BOOK 2

CHAPTER 19

I spent the first few years after marrying Charlie running from my path. I wanted a normal life. We moved from York to Mechanicsburg, a small train station town, as Charlie liked to call it. I didn't do yoga. I didn't meditate. I didn't do intuitive readings, hypnotherapy or Reiki except for close friends and Hope and Charlie. However, when life wants to find you, it does.

Instead, during that time, I spent time at work and with my daughter, as Charlie's job had him away for weeks at a time. I started by getting random calls from a couple of people in different states saying they were referred to me. I started having more friends and friends of friends and co-workers asking for hypnotherapy sessions and intuitive readings. If I didn't sink back into my path, which was not just calling me, but screaming loudly to accept who I was, I knew it would somehow in a big way catch up with me. I've learned in so many ways that when you don't go with the flow of the universe, it will bring you to your knees until you do.

I did however, have an incessant need for keeping myself busy, coupled with a determination that I could attribute to the influence of my mother's immigrant family. It seems that immigrants work extra hard to make a new life. My influences—my aunts and uncles, worked long grueling days to give their children a good life. This was not lost on me.

In addition to my day job, I had opened an organic clothing store, joined several non-profit boards, and produced a Women's Day event for three years in celebration of International Women's Day. The event, "Rock the Sisterhood," gave women an opportunity to share stories, history while creating art, healing through holistic medicine and more. One year I moved it to the town where I lived after the non-profit I partnered with was undergoing changes in its mission and future.

"That was great! Could you bring that here more often or permanently, Susan?" I heard from people in the community. I looked at the yoga teacher next to me and said, "What do you think? Would you teach yoga for me?"

I was an on and off again yogini in no way qualified to teach. But I could offer my services of Hypnotherapy and Reiki. I soon moved my clothing store down the street and in the old space where we started the clothing store. I opened *Barefoot Yoga and Wellness Studio.*

It was named such because as soon as you opened the door, you had to remove your shoes as you were in the tiny classroom that couldn't hold more than six people. Shortly after opening, we added a massage therapist and acupuncturist. Within a few months, we outgrew our space and moved, continuing to grow.

While my professional life continued to grow, my personal life started to collapse. What Charlie and I didn't understand was that the government didn't like someone traveling back and forth between countries. Charlie had to choose. He needed to stay in Canada or he needed to apply for his Visa and live here for at least six months out of the year. Each cross of the border back into the U.S. traumatized him. He was fingerprinted, held in enclosed rooms, questioned about his work, our marriage, his intentions. After each visit, we realized we had to keep documentation about his life. He would lug back and forth a binder of his high school and college records, our marriage certificate, photos of us and one with us and Hope. Finally, one trip back home, he was detained for hours and refused at the border.

We didn't see each other for almost three months while he went through the process of applying for a Visa. Just because you marry an American citizen doesn't make you eligible for living in the states. When I was younger, it seemed so easy for my family to move here just because other families did. All of that had changed with 9/11. The border was more secure. Guards were more on edge.

When Charlie arrived home, Visa in hand, he walked through the door with a bushy mountain-man beard. He refused to trim his beard in depression of waiting to come home.

At first, we rejoiced in seeing one another. He struggled with how to get film jobs here and what he should do with his career. We then battled a childhood nemesis of mine—alcoholism. The first year we were together, I didn't realize how much he drank. My experience with alcoholics was people who turned violent, aggressive, and went constantly to a bar. Charlie was, in a sense, a functioning alcoholic. He didn't go to bars. He drank at home and often, mostly when I was not at home. Being together regularly now brought this to my attention.

At first he didn't agree with my assessment. He said he could stop and only have one drink every evening. Slowly one drink would turn into an entire bottle and he couldn't stop. He lied about when he was drunk. I could tell by his voice, his walk, and that silent odor only those who've lived with alcoholics can smell a mile away.

He went through the struggles every alcoholic went through. He denied his addiction. He tried to deal with it himself. He went to AA. He fell off the wagon. Finally, one day, he managed to make it to the next, and then the next. He cleaned empty and partially full bottles of booze he would hide around the house where I could not find them. He made amends with those he hurt.

We moved Barefoot in with an art studio that recently had several art studios available and a large floor to teach classes. A short while after moving in, a talented yoga teacher at my studio told me I was ready to start teaching yoga. I stepped my foot into the water, relishing this amazing experience. Soon after, I started teaching meditation classes, as well. My path continued to take twists and turns, but all leading me to the same destination. That path took another turn, leading us to move the studio one more time. A two hundred-year-old farmhouse surrounded by acres of land and nearby farmland was for rent. A friend and I scouted out the place one evening, holding hands above our eyes trying to peak into the windows. I called the landlord that evening and within a few weeks, we moved in.

Surrounded by grass, wild plants, deer running through the land, we utilized the space outside for Reiki attunements and Tai Chi classes. Inside we held yoga classes, had rooms for massage and acupuncture, and I was back to doing intuitive readings. Arabella had reminded me that I was given this gift for a reason. I should be using it.

CHAPTER 20

The Great Awakening

In 2011, a shift occurred. A shift to me is when spirit alters something in your energy field. When I get shifts, I usually feel like something has changed inside of my energy field. I can feel the energy around me and inside me. It's like you wake up one morning and know something is different. These didn't happen during my sleep, but rather me standing somewhere and suddenly I know something has changed. Imagine you wake up with the color of your hair mysteriously being different. Before you look in the mirror, you know something has changed. When you finally see it, your gut instinct makes sense.

Most times, shifts were done slowly over the course of few days. Sometimes they were done through spirit and other times I sought them out through "attunements," which are energy changes when studying the healing arts. A Reiki practitioner receives "attunements" (or adjustments to their energy field) in order to provide healing energy.

In the late winter, I went through a shift. It took a few weeks to settle in. During this time, I cried and thought I was losing my mind. Everything was confusing. Although I was already extremely intuitive, I felt more so. Whenever I had a shift, that survival part of me kicked in and I thought I was going to die. Poor Arabella would get so many calls from me during these times.

"Do you have any feelings about me?" I would ask. "Do you think I am going to die soon?

After getting me off the ledge, she would say that she didn't. For many years, my reaction was always the same—impending death. Which really wasn't far off, just misplaced. Whenever anything changes, it goes through a death. Something old disappears while something new grows.

At this time, I didn't know how I could possibly get anymore intuitive from a change. I'm sure my guides must laugh when I say this. After this particular one, I felt more deeply everything around me. My sixth sense was heightened. I felt a need to be available to those who needed me. I wasn't sure what this was about until my best friend, Kat, looked ill at work one day.

Kat had entered my life moving back to Pennsylvania from her travels living in California and New England. She was an herbalist and also intuitive. Like all of my close friends, this Pisces, wiggled her way into my life through working where I did and wooing me with holistic talk. That day in particular I asked her what was going on.

"I just feel off. I don't know what's going on with me. I feel like I've been losing my mind."

By that time, "they" (the other side) told me that those that were here to lead the way to a great change were being awakened. It was like taking an entire group of robots and turning them all on so they could go out into the world and be ready to help when something big happened. (What I did not know then was that there was indeed about to be a global change.)

Kat shared the same symptoms—migraines, fatigue, feeling run down and then just the weird mental issues. Her energy felt off. I told her about my experience and what "they" told me. This gave her comfort. I was able to then be there as I saw spiritual friend, one after another, suddenly move through this energetic awakening.

As the weather warmed, I sat outside as much as I could. I was naturally an outdoors person, but I felt the earth calling. I would sit with my palms pressed to Mother Earth and hear her call. Except now, she had quite enough. She said something was going to change. I had never felt her this way. Usually she was soft, intense and loving. She felt raped by the world. It was like a mother who stayed home with the children all day and after months threw up her hands and said, "I need a break!"

Another co-worker, Char, knew a healer in Baltimore. After many times of saying, "let's go," I took her up on it. Char and I made our way down to his apartment. It was like meeting the oracle in the movie *The Matrix.* The neighborhood wasn't the best. Outside and inside of the apartment one could feel the energy of danger mingled with the graffiti and trash lining the streets. One foot into Angel's apartment, and suddenly you were in another world. It was so peaceful.

Each sunrise and sunset, Angel performs an ancient Vedic fire ceremony. Using a pyramid shaped copper vessel known as an agnihotra, he performs this ceremony to purify the air and bring peace. People from all over the world perform the lighting of rice, ghee (Indian clarified butter), dried cow dung chips, and say sanskrit mantras.

We missed the sunset fire ceremony, but Angel kindly repeated it for us so we could have the experience. While Char had been to Angel before and knew of this ceremony, this was my first time witnessing it. I could see through the flames. I could see the fire itself as a life force. I looked at Angel and said, "You were a solider in past lives in an Asian army, hundreds of years ago."

He then said, "You were a shaman. You have Native American energy all around you."

I hopped onto his massage table situated in what would have been the middle of his Dining/Living Room. He started his healing session, which was very influenced by native traditions, and used a sage smudge stick, native words and sounds. He told me I had beautiful energy and I needed to use my voice. "Your voice has healing energy. You need to sing. Your singing opens people's hearts."

Before Charlie and I were together I used to sing in coffee shops sporadically with different musicians. I hadn't sung since the year before, when in Canada, I met a yoga teacher who was instructing me on how to sing mantras. I started learning them and using them during my yoga classes.

He also told me I had a Shaman guide who was with me. He said I needed more prayer and meditation because people will come to me. "Go to the mountains and be quiet. Do your ceremony and see the Indian who is with you."

Angel continued, "Every time you help someone, it lights your heart up. Your purpose in life is to heal."

"There is more to you than meets the eye. You have psychic ability since you were six or seven years old. You have an angelic way about you. You are full of love, unconditional love. "

Angel also knew I wanted to do a book. He told me to have a child-like attitude and no ego for heaven was at hand. I had many book ideas, one that I had abandoned years ago. I started writing about my dating life as a therapeutic approach to surviving the dating world. I had also had the idea of a story from when Charlie and I were married in Salem.

Char, Angel and I ended the evening with a cup of what I believe was twig tea, also known as Kukicha. Made of stems, stalks and twigs of tea shrubs, this Japanese blend had a woody taste, as you could imagine. I found it interesting that after an evening of energy work, he knew what would be best for a drive home—giving us literally the earth so we could "ground" ourselves.

The concept of "grounding" is simple. When you are too much in your head or perhaps your upper chakras (like your throat, third eye and crown), you need to get yourself in touch with the world you live in. Some use walking, gardening, hiking, or even visualizing roots extending from the feet into the ground. Simply eating or drinking a "grounding" food, however, can also be just as beneficial.

In the spring, Char and I took our next adventure to South Street in Philadelphia to enjoy window-shopping, hop into the holistic bookstore there and see a psychic. As we walked along South Street, I paused.

"Are you OK, Susan?"

In a moment that seemed like minutes had flown by, I had a sudden download of energy come in through the crown of my head. It poured in with white and blue light making me quite dizzy. I could only see the colors coming straight down through me and feel the abundant sensations of love and intensity. When it passed, all I could say was, "Cool!" This was the first time I had a shift happen so obvious, holding my complete attention with me knowing exactly what was going on.

After my shift, angels started to become more present in my life once again. My buddy Michael had taken a gracious exit from my life, as I was preoccupied with other interests. However, he was back again, making his presence known (and always wanting to look good for when the right occasion came about). Ariel came through teaching me about the spirit of animals and nature. And Jophiel guided me to acting jobs and literally came along for many rides while I drove to Pittsburgh and West Virginia for work.

One evening, Arabella asked where Archangel Gabriel was, as he had not visited her in a few days. She had started to have a multitude of angel experiences. Moments later my German shepherd, Madison, barked at a large shadowy outline of a being that filled my kitchen. The figure said, "I am here." *Hello, Gabriel,* I thought. Those angels, always cracking jokes.

CHAPTER 21

The Political Game

In 2008, I was encouraged to run for the local state
Senate race for the Democrats. I had jumped parties
several times growing up, was clearly a liberal, and had no
idea how I would win. However, the local group told me
that as a community leader (I was on several local boards),
I could potentially sway voters. My campaign motto was
"We Believe in Susan Kiskis," a play on the new *Batman*
movie that was just released.

I ran in a conservative area against an incumbent that
the people loved. I didn't stand a chance.

Not knowing this though, I went all in. I held campaign
fundraisers, went door knocking, made phone calls, made
appearances, and hoped my unstable childhood would not
make its way into dirty politics. I decided if I was going to
try, I really would. Charlie canvased for me, covering entire
communities with door hangers. He was my biggest fan.

I learned people's names, their spouse's names, their
kids' names, their dogs' names. As someone who did not
remember names well, this was a huge skill for me to
learn. I studied Pennsylvania history, my opponent's voting
record, current laws being considered. I jammed my brain
with as much as I thought I would need.

Instead of finding joy in the race like my mother did
(who told me politics was in our family's blood), I felt
isolated and phony. Luckily, my childhood and family was
not dragged through the mud. With a drug addict brother
who had a record, a mother who by then had also been in
jail, and a father who had been arrested countless times
for spousal abuse, I was an easy target, I either seemed

like no threat at all or the incumbent, who I heard later was pro-woman, chose restraint over attacking a fellow woman. I was blessed. I lost, but my image was not tarnished.

When running for politics, you have to present yourself in a certain way to get elected. Wearing suits and kissing babies—no problem, that was not a stretch for me at all. Toeing the line on being more conservative than I was felt like a lie. Let's face it. I am a tree-hugging, gay-loving, equal rights, all natural, granola kind of girl. I believe in term limits. I believe that people should pay school taxes to support our public school system and educate the next generation. I was in no way qualified to meet the criteria for this area. Even though we would be dealing with state issues, people only wanted to know if you met their top three national criteria. 1) Where do you stand on abortion? 2) Are you a Republican? 3) Do you believe in taxes? If you could not answer correctly to even one of those questions, there would be no way to make it into a conversation or leave a door hanger.

I had been working for a newspaper that I decided to leave the month before the November election. My day was sometimes filled with up to nineteen hours of working and on the "campaign trail." I was exhausted. After I lost, Charlie told me to take time to recoup and to do things I wanted to do.

My time led me to doing extra work on films. I also took the clothing store on the road to various festivals. Within a few months, I was also on the hook for running for local council.

Local council races were much more laid back and easier to manage. Many people in the community knew me from my activities in town or my recent race. Those who were on the other political side had less concern for crossing over to vote for me for the local race. I managed to get my name listed on both tickets in the fall. I won easily.

Time off of work took its toll on our finances. We quickly drained our bank accounts. Charlie's parents helped us not lose our house, which at one point had gone into foreclosure. The economy was rough. Our businesses made little and I could not get a job. I was either overqualified for jobs or competing against those who were overqualified for the jobs I was applying for. Layoffs over the past few years had me now competing with CEOs and VPs for management positions. Interviews were a nightmare, hearing both of these reasons tossed back at me. I finally got a job working at a health food store right before the November elections for local council.

A New Teacher

The old saying, "When the student is ready, the teacher will come," could not be truer. I found that spirit knows exactly when and where to place that special teacher.

Sometimes in our lives we will find a person that will touch our lives deeply, teaching us what we were seeking or perhaps things we didn't know we needed to know. A good book could unravel our minds. Even a spirit guide can come through, teaching us if we are willing to listen.

In the fall, a gentleman by the name of David entered my life with no notice. One day, I woke up wanting to know New Paradigm Multi-Dimensional Transformation (also known as MDT and formerly known as Shamballa Reiki). In over ten years of practicing Usui Reiki, I never knew much about MDT nor ever had the desire to learn about it. MDT is different than Usui Reiki. Most people are introduced to Reiki via the Usui form—the one I call "the light and fluffy love-Reiki." When I used it, that's what it felt like to me—soft, gentle, and safe. MDT was a whole other ball of wax.

I joined David for MDT attunements at a space he was teaching at in Harrisburg. During MDT training, I learned what it was through experience. It felt more aggressive, stronger. My first experience in class surrounded me with angels during our meditation and attunement process. I was surrounded by them: ancestors, guides, a wolf, and a bear. They pushed me into nothingness, except a space of purple light. I felt alone, hesitant and then the sensation of enormous energy running through my body. Peace and stillness met me shortly thereafter. Before me, Pegasus appeared, lifting into flight as Mother Earth below separated, showing me that any conflict Charlie and I were creating in this life was karma we were creating now, not from past lives.

David instructed us to hold and move our chi. I started to turn my hands back and forth, spaced a few inches from each other, as if I was moving a ball in my hands exercising my wrists. The energy became so intense I thought I was going to jump out of my body. Even when he said to turn our palms down towards our knees, the energy stayed strong. I became fearful once again; a part of me cried that it was too much. I next heard a voice, "This energy is in you. What you feel in your hands is yours to give."

I knew in that moment that death creates growth. Energy was like a plant dying and then feeding the nutrients in the earth for the next thing to grow from it. After our attunement, a fellow student and I were giving each other Reiki, as per David's request. She told me "they" were repairing the right side of my body, sewing it up. The right side of one's body is the masculine side. Someone from the other side was helping to heal my damaged masculine side. David then came over and said he saw me shape-shift into a swan. During my session, I saw India and a man meditating. I pulled the energy I felt running through me, visualizing and feeling it move up my spine until I felt taller and more peaceful.

After my first attunement, I cried for hours. As to why I was crying, I had no idea. It seems like in our country, crying is something that we do when we are weak. It is to be avoided at all costs, particularly in public. However, crying is a natural function of the body. It enables us to let go, releasing pent up, sometimes unconscious, feelings. I have seen countless people cry during Reiki sessions, attunements, yoga classes, intuitive readings, and more. We all seem to have this mask we wear held so tightly over our true selves that any time we start to let go of our fast-paced lives based on the expectations we or others have for us, brings on the tears. It becomes a release, an emotional detox if you will. Kind of like sweating, which no one seems to like, either. I accepted my tears.

For days after the first attunement, I had dreams of purple and blue fire. David mentioned how MDT was associated with St. Germaine and the violet flame.

As the attunements progressed, we learned how to send Reiki to those far away from us (across space), but across time, as well. This was something that was not foreign to me as I had learned this from Karen when taking Usui Reiki. Shamans use this technique to heal trauma in early life.

In this class, we sent Reiki through any time, past, present or future. We learned muscle testing, applied kinesiology. This process helps you get feedback from your body that your mind may not be aware of. In one form, you touch your index and thumb together. Next you loop your right and left fingers together. With correct questions, your fingers stay locked. If it is a false answer, they break apart.

Another way is by standing up with knees bent. You begin to ask questions you know answers to. Your body will naturally sway forward to back for correct answers. If I said, "*My name is Susan*" or "*I was born in NYC*" for me, my correct answers would sway my body forward. If I said, "*I like spicy foods,*" my body would sway back. Your body becomes like a pendulum.

In future attunements, I saw the Buddhist deity Tara, turquoise and sea green light descending into me from the top of my head, gold-plated books that represented the akashic records. I felt myself surrounded by Archangels Michael and Uriel, and I felt the presence of God.

Having all of these experiences had been something I was able to do since I was a child. Their validity was not in question for me. I didn't need to prove them to know they were real to me. However, my mind, always focused on the scientific answers for *why* and *how* was always spinning. I always kept looking for research. However, living in a world dominated by our five limited senses, made it difficult.

Why is it so out of question that we can see things that are not "there?" We live in a three dimensional world where we mostly only see two dimensions. Science has shown that there are upwards of ten to eleven dimensions. Humans only see the visible spectrum, just a small portion of the electromagnetic spectrum. Other species see other colors that we cannot see. We can only hear certain frequencies, associated with our human vocals. We cannot hear the sound of a dog whistle. These thoughts helped shape my ability to explain to others what made this real for me, why I could believe.

Following MDT, I joined David's class on Munay Ki Rites. What I did not know was that after a year of talking to angels (which had not occurred since I was a child), "they" decided that it was time to go back to the shaman. A few years ago, I became immersed in Native American studies, drumming, and more. When I met a deep intuitive, they would always as me if I was Native, or if I had a past life as a Native, or if I had a Native guide (just like Angel did). I started to bond with my native spirit guide, receiving guidance from him in my dreams and in my waking moments.

For six months I studied with David an Incan Shamanic Healing, known as Munay Ki Rites. Usui Reiki is the light fluffy Reiki to me because to me it is soft, inviting, safe and full of pink unconditional love. MDT has always appeared to me purple—the violet flame, as it is known— intense and very effective for deep healing and "cleaning house." Munay Ki had my body feeling hot like a flame; I also felt encompassed in love, and was not without a visitor or several.

In Munay Ki Rites, there are different levels of "attunements," known as "rites." Each level provided its own set of experiences for me. In one, I felt the room full of ancestors. I didn't think it could get anymore packed in this small office, but there they were excitedly and proudly standing in every inch behind us, above us, on us. This form of energy work was taught to anthropologist, Alberto Villoldo, while he studied with the Q'ero shamans in Peru. It was meant as an introduction for those starting on their path as a shaman (healer).

During the "Seer's Rites" I felt like my mind was going to explode with information. On one hand, part of my mind knew what I was being given through spirit, but on the other hand, my mind was so limited it could not hold and understand it. To me the Seer's Rite was trying to not think about something I could not understand. I had to let whatever information my subconscious mind needed soak in quietly. The funny thing was how prior to the Seer's Rite I thought, *How could I possibly know anymore than I already know?* So, much for that thought!

After practicing and working with Munay Ki, the ancestors never went away, but the angels and other guides came back talking and teaching small lessons. Then, without warning, the shaman came back. This time he came back reminding me of a previous life as a shaman.

One day, I was sitting outside on my back porch enjoying the evening and my garden. The mantra "I remember," came to my mind and my lips without ceasing. I repeated over and over again *I remember.* I then consciously formed my own mantra, "What do I remember?"

I saw the head of the chief or shaman one day with a feathered headdress and yellow feathers for eyelashes. I saw him another time standing tall, wearing an entire costume made of yellow feathers. What these visions meant, I did not know. But I did know that with careful listening, every day a new piece of the puzzle would appear either through a vision from my Native friend or from the words of people I meet every day. My friend Sara, who taught at my yoga studio, told me that she received a message for me in her meditation one day. "Your lesson right now is to share the medicine you have learned—to pass it to future generations."

When we think of medicine, we think of Western medicine and pharmaceuticals. And then there is the Eastern form of Chinese Medicine and Ayurveda, and indigenous herbal medicine. That message from Sara was about sharing the medicine of life—like knowing that while life leads us around twists and bends, we can remember who we truly are regardless of nature or nurture. Our true self, our essence, lies within our bones and retains the knowledge we have gained from centuries of lives. The knowledge we build within this lifetime continues to help achieve whatever it is we are meant to do.

While I instinctively knew who the man in my vision was. I needed time for my rational mind sort it out and "prove" what my gut knew. I saw myself. I was a chief in a past life. I was a shaman. It was one of the only explanations for explaining how I knew how to work a hand drum with little guidance. How instinctively native sounds echoed from my lips when I smudged a room or held my drum, just like Spanish words did (which I was to discover later why). It connected my bond to the earth, my respect for animals, my need to use natural remedies from plants.

My next journey led me to an Egyptian form of Reiki, Sekhem Seikem. Founded by Patrick Zeigler while spending a night in the pyramid of Giza, Sekhem Seikem connects with the Egyptian priests and priestesses and healing energy long forgotten.

During the first attunement, I saw an image of a woman with lines of paint across her cheeks, wearing beads around her neck, and donning a headdress. I shared with David who indicated that this could be a vision of the embalming process used by Egyptians that I was witnessing. Death was around me again, showing me its face once again, symbolizing change. I had another woman present me with a ball of light after I felt the energy, like the sun itself move down through my spinal column, sway back and forth from side to side and shoot straight up out of my head back to the sky.

At the second attunement, I was shown a vision I had previously seen. Me and my mountain. Not my mountain, but a dark gray mountain where there was no time. On this mountain I stood in my cloak and observed, waiting, and when the time was right took souls to the other side. This was the place I go to when I take a vacation from incarnations, I realized. Sounds pleasant, doesn't it? Here I thought a vacation would be me sitting on a beach on a lounge chair drinking a margarita without a care in the world. Instead, I go to a mountainous resort where I stand as the grim-reaper taking souls when it is their time to go. No wonder I loved the grim reaper in *Bill and Ted's Excellent Adventure*. I remember being so enamored by him, laughing to myself, thinking I must be a grim reaper. Here, my "job" on the other side was revealed, indicating that's exactly what I do. I was the Grim Reaper when not on an incarnation binge. And here in my second attunement in Sekhem Seikem and they were giving me a reminder. Ironic that I fear death when the information I had been presented was that I was in essence, death itself.

"Everyone has a parent angel," my friend Arabella told me once.

With this new discovery, I wondered who mine was. Surely Michael was way too casual with me to by my "boss" if you will. He was more like my mentor, my confident. However, if I was going to a mountain to retrieve souls when it was time, I knew who my supervisor was—Azrael. Upon that thought, I saw him smile a big, scary smile like Azrael, the cat from *Smurfs*. And, I would find out soon enough, he had a job for me.

In the third attunement of Sekhem Seikem, I felt like butterflies floated through me in every direction, which opened to a vision of a falcon. The falcon had a partial kill in its mouth and was in turn eaten by a snake nearby. The snake released waste from its body onto rocks, which then made its way into the water. This fed other life along with created other life. Everything feeds into everything. Everything is connected. And perhaps in death, souls can also give up their self-identity and instead of be individual beings like I have met, become part of the energy of the world, feeding everyone. Everything needs to be nourished.

CHAPTER 22

Blue Jay

While still managing multiple businesses and working full time, my father, who had been in a nursing home for over five years, began to decline dramatically. One day the nurse told my mother, "He's in the dying process."

It was confusing at first because nothing health-wise had changed. My father had diabetes and was thin as a rail, always wanting a nurse to wheel him outside for a smoke ten times a day, but nothing else was wrong that doctors could find. Perhaps the will to live had just ceased.

He started telling my mother he saw his mother, who died when I was a child, in the room. My dad slept more than usual. He became less engaged with visitors and started to forget names. For two months we watched his body and mind come to a close. Every day we wondered if today was the day my father was going to die. Two weeks before he crossed over, my mother and I visited him every day. He kept plugging along much to the shock of hospice nurses. I sat with him and did Reiki on him. I read him articles written by Buddhist monks and writers. In his waking conscious, he would never allow me to do this. When his mind started to go, he would wake, waving me away when I tried. But in his final days, he did nothing. So, I read. I did Reiki. I prayed.

His room was full of spirits until the last few days and then suddenly it became quiet. I knew the time was close. My mother, brother, his partner, their son and I all were there. I said my goodbyes to my father whose body had started to shut down the day before. I scooped up my nephew and took him to the lounge. I didn't think a three-year-old should see the trauma of human emotions that filled the room. I sat him on my lap, feeding him candy and talking about happy things. I felt my dad pass away (which I knew would happen as soon as we left the room). I gave my nephew a big hug and explained to him what was happening and how we still live on, just not in a way we are used to seeing. In the room, my dad was gone. A body lay in his place, but he was no longer there. My mother came over to me to tell me he passed just a few short minutes after my nephew and I entered the lounge.

I remembered going to a wake one time for Kevin's grandfather. It was my first experience around a body. I couldn't understand why people did this. It was so unnerving. That person was not there. There was no energy from that being under the makeup and suit. I swore I'd never go again, but did to honor my Uncle Kola when he passed.

I quickly started gathering up all of my father's personal belonging inserting them into my car and all the while coordinating with the nursing home and funeral home what to do next. I was in my own personal shock mode. Getting everything done, taking care of what was needed, and holding things together was my way of surviving. My mother was collapsed on a chair and my brother and his family had departed soon after my father exhaled his last breath.

On one of my trips to my car, piling in my dad's life, I finally broke down. There he was, standing near me. Happy, standing tall, the man I called my father looked at me with love. He felt like pure joy. He felt good, healthy.

"Oh God, Dad. I love you. I am so sorry. I miss you," I sobbed.

"Take care of your mother," he told me. My father loved my mother like there was no other person in the world. Despite all of his flaws, her flaws, the mess of their relationship, he loved her unconditionally, even in death.

After the initial visit, my father came to see my mother and I several times. It made her frightened because he seemed angry and unsettled. She was unable to understand how souls need to examine their life after they pass and Dad had done some awful things he could not remember when he was drunk. Of course it was difficult. If someone showed you a video of all of the nasty, crazy things you did during your lifetime, you would be angry and unsettled, too.

Eventually his visits softened and became less in number. One time in a dream I was in a coffee shop and saw my dad outside. I ran to the door and each of us with a hand on the door wanting to say hello. I put my other hand on the glass, trying to reach out to him. I could not open the door. I cried, wanting to be near him. The door was the veil that separated the worlds and I could not cross it.

My father started appearing to my mother as a blue bird. My mother, who grew up on a farm, hated nature. She however, loved animals (feeding even the squirrels and the possums in her tiny yard). With her failing vision, it was hard for her to see anything, not being able to sometimes decipher between a possum and cat. In her neighborhood, she had the typical house finches and sparrows, but that was all. Until one day a blue bird showed up and she knew that was my father.

CHAPTER 23

Nimue

A year after my father passed Charlie and I went to Rhode Island to pick up my daughter from her adventure at summer camp for smart kids. During the weekend visit, we stopped by Sleepy Hollow in New York since they were both horror film fans.

During a hot humid Saturday, we entered the Sleepy Hollow Cemetery that was not only the final resting place of historical figures, but contained the bridge of the headless horseman. Under the bridge ran the Pocantico River, shallow and narrow in this spot. Walking along the river two deer spooked by us, and our dogs took off, but then suddenly stopped. While one of the deer turned away from us, the other stood, locked in a gaze with me. I shifted my energy to connect with the deer standing not so far away.

In this moment, I felt words and sounds form in my mouth. I heard myself saying, "Nimue" (Nimway) with no realization of what I was saying. The space was filled with a sense of understanding, as if saying, "We are at peace. I acknowledge the space between us, around us." I saw pink light, the color of love for me, near the deer and myself. Before walking away, I consciously said my greeting to all animals, plants and earth, "I see you," my version of the Hindi word, "Jai."

While the encounter only lasted a few minutes, I felt compelled to spend part of the ride back home looking up on my phone what "Nimue" was. I assumed it must have been a Native American word based on my recent studies in Shamanism. I found that the Pocantico River, which runs through a hamlet of the same name, was originally settled by Native Americans of the Wecquaesgeek tribes. Perhaps they gave me the word. I closely relate meanings of animal encounters to Native tribal stories. However, I Googled the word and the assumed cultural reference, only to keep getting website after website of references to Celtic lore.

Nimue was another name for the Lady of the Lake in Arthurian Legends with Scottish and Welsh background. It is thought to also be related to the Celtic Goddess Nemetona/Niniane/Nemain of the sacred grove and protector of sacred places and forests.

Charlie who is of the earth always surprises me. He said out of the blue later in the evening, that perhaps the word came to me because in this amazing landscape, we were walking through the Sleepy Hollow cemetery where many Scots, Irish, and British ancestors lay. He thought it would be natural they would give me a reference to their heritage (and mine) as a means of communicating.

In even the most surprising places, even when we don't expect it, our intuition can take us to magical places. There was a reason the deer stopped for us. The encounter of speaking to the deer with my mind, words and energy was unexpected. In this place where bodies rested before their journey home, I never expected to have ancestors find me and create such a beautiful moment.

In finding this Celtic connection, I felt my mind draw to Kat. She would be heading to Ireland in a few days. Deer is her totem and upon speaking with her later, she said she was asking for safe passage over the water. Perhaps they heard her prayer.

As we walked back to the car that day, I wondered if my father was there with us. A short while after the thought crossed my mind, we passed headstones of a Murphy family (my maiden name). I nodded at dad. And a little farther out, I paused for a moment as we passed another headstone of a James Alexander (my father's first and last name). My dad was there in this historical place showing me more than the tombs of Rockefeller, Carnegie and Irving. He reminded me of the endless connection of life.

CHAPTER 24

I Want to Stay

"I want to stay," I said. Nathan Lane started waving his wand around. Sparkles of silver light flashed around like he was a fairy godmother granting a wish.

"I want to stay... here... on Earth!" I shouted, stomping my feet on the soft ground for good measure. When you ask for something, I learned, you have to be specific. I almost missed that. *Here* could have been heaven, or somewhere caught in-between. I needed to make sure God and I were on the same page.

As Nathan Lane did his thing, I felt this vortex of white light, flecks of pastel pinks, blues and purples surround me. I was being lifted off the ground, felt like my insides were pouring out into a funnel of all loving, all encompassing peace, until there was me, and nothing of me. It was as if I was everything and nothing all at once. And then I woke up.

I only knew I was alive when I woke up. I took a moment to make sure that I was truly in my house and not a figment of my dead imagination. I even pinched myself to make sure.

I stood, out of bed, wondering if God really understood my decision, or if I was going to drop dead in five minutes. I went from elated to have made "the right decision," to consumed with relief. My soul decided to stay. I wanted my mind to be present when this day came about again, by my soul wanted to stay. Whew!

I then remembered that there was more than just the vortex and me waking up. I had knowledge that was pressed into my subconscious waiting to be discovered. I tried pulling it out to no avail. So, I sat. I sat like Buddha, contemplating and letting go simultaneously.

What I remembered was this, 1) I resolved the karma I wanted to resolve in its most basic form in this life. 2) I could have left, fulfilling exactly what needed to be fulfilled. 3) By staying, I was saying that I was willing to dive deeper into the lessons my soul wanted to explore.

I told my husband Charlie what had happened. He didn't like it so much. "Why would you want to go? Why would you want to leave me?"

"It's not about whether I wanted to leave you or not, it was a bigger decision than that. But yay, I chose to stay, and I wasn't even conscious when I made that decision, so that means I really wanted to stay!" I replied.

"But you almost didn't. You needed to think about it."

"Don't you see? It's like I finished a marathon and I could retire knowing what I accomplished or I could see what life is like after a marathon, perhaps even do another," I said proudly. Happiness was lost on Charlie.

Rather than thinking what was next, instead, I thought about the silence I felt. The stillness that lived within my being was reward enough. What I didn't know was that karma phase two was right around the corner.

CHAPTER 25

Grandma & Grandpa

Nathan Lane, however, was not my trigger for how my two years of major spiritual growth happened. In fact, I know the exact moment that changed everything. Snuggled in bed on a cool Autumn evening in 2012, my maternal grandparents, Katrina and George (whom I never met in person since they lived in Montenegro), paid me a visit.

In a state of sleep, I entered a space where it was as if my eyes were open and I could see my room clearly. I felt a presence coming from the corner of my room that would not stop its progression even though I prayed. I silently called out a powerful mantra Arabella shared with me, "God, send a legion of angels to protect me." This was followed by my typical mantra that "If you are not from God, you will not be able to come to me," and "God, please take this being and wash them in your light and love and only then if they are from you, can they approach me." At the foot of my bed, the silhouette of a purple light, an angel sat. That still however, did not stop the presence from approaching.

My body started to shake in fear. Then, suddenly, the presence appeared in its human forms. It was my grandparents. My grandmother who was closest to me, my timid grandfather behind her, did not speak a word. Instead, Katrina pushed her pointed index finger into the side of my head.

I woke up. I woke Charlie up. What was wrong with me? Was I going to die? (Do you see a theme here?) After a fretful night with little sleep, I spent the next twenty-four hours consumed with fear. I picked Arabella's brain. I asked my daughter to "read" me (giving me an intuitive reading). I finally called Joy, a friend who was a ThetaHealing practitioner.

Recounting the story, I held back my questions until her intuition was taking too long. I could not afford the seconds to tap into the collective unconscious. I asked her if I was going to die.

"Yes, but not now," she said with a snicker. "The angels are laughing that you forget you will die someday. But today is not the day," said Joy.

She then led me through an applied kinesiology technique that David taught me—where you stand up with knees bent and sway your body front-to-back to get answers.

"My name is Susan Kiskis." My body swayed forward.

"I live in Pennsylvania." Once again I shifted forward.

"I am a rock star." And back my body went.

After a round of basic questions, we found my yes and no. Joy then started asking the deeper questions allowing my body to simply answer. Within ten minutes, Joy had enough information to tell me her conclusion.

"They changed your DNA. It would be like what we do during a ThetaHealing attunement or what you see with the Mystery School DNA activation."

"Why?"

"It's a way to have your body be more in touch with your light body. That and perhaps if you had any pre-dispositioned diseases in your family, they took them away."

Your light body is what it sounds like—a version of you, but pure light. Imagine for a moment that you are energy and that energy is pure light. When you incarnate on earth, your consciousness, the energy of you, lives inside a body of matter. However, you are still a being of light. So, you have all of these other "bodies," parts made of energy that you may choose to access in this life. Imagine them all benefiting you in different ways—helping your emotions, your physical body, and your spiritual connection. Have you ever heard the term aura? Aura is one of your closest energy bodies clinging onto the outside of the physical body. You may have heard someone say how your aura is pink or blue. A light body is farther away from your physical body, but let's say it is the one thing you really want to work on bringing towards your physical being. With your light body, you may have more clarity, purpose, and connection to serving others than oneself. The story that's going around in the New Age world is how our world's energy is changing, and so, we are modifying ourselves to bring in this Light Body, to bring in more energy and ultimately serve the greater good.

With Joy having calmed my tornado of thoughts, my mind became still. And then I realized, I had another shift.

CHAPTER 26

All About Bob

Arabella started receiving special visits from an unknown character on the other side. Bob wanted to listen to "Rocket Man" by Sir Elton John, while riding in the car. He obviously did not need the air bag on, and only when Arabella was driving by herself, with Bob, did the passenger air bag light go off on its own.

She told me about this mysterious visitor who wanted to listen to specific music, asking me to hone in on who he was. Bob didn't give me a human form as I introduced myself (which was typical for me during the early stages of meeting spirit guides). He provided an outline filled in by white and blue light. He jokingly said, "Call me Bob." I find many times that guides and angels will alter whether they show you a form that is human-like or just light (what seems to be our pure state). I knew Bob was male, easy going, had a sense of humor, and kind. He seemed to surround Arabella with a sense of peace. When she would be introduced to heavy hitter guides or angels with serious messages, Bob melted into the background keeping things light.

Recently, however, Arabella awoke with a dream, saying, "Maclellan." She wanted to start her day, but he would not let her—until she knew more about him. He definitively told her he was a Scot—not Irish. He showed her his face with a blazing red beard. Later that day, she texted me saying, "I know who my guide is!"

I called her and she said she looked up a Bob Maclellan from Scotland online and found a few. She was not sure which one he was yet, but he told her it took her long enough to figure out who he was (since he said, he was with her since she was 17, after her mother passed away).

I said to her I felt like Bob was old, perhaps a few hundred years old. I wondered why a soul that old would not have reincarnated. Immediately, I got the feeling like recovery. He said it was like he was a member of AA (Alcoholics Anonymous) and was still recovering. He also said he was making amends for the past. Not that he had to, but that he wanted to.

Upon passing along the message, Arabella said, "Well, thank you for the confirmation." She had found a Robert Maclellan from the 1600's that lead a less than stellar life. She felt like he was doing some sort of penance. The Robert Maclellan she found died in 1641 and was the Provost of Kirkcudbright and known for violence. I mentioned to her that I still also think that aside from the analogy, he may have been a fan of booze and women.

Before Bob stepped in to tell me more about his motives for not reincarnating, Arabella asked me if people could become guides when they pass over. When my first dog, Lucky, a Maltese, passed, it was my first experience with death from the start of the death process to crossing over to the other side.

Lucky was an ill, senior dog with a notch in his throat and could barely eat or drink anymore. He was weak and wasting away. My mother made the difficult decision (with advisement from the veterinarian), to euthanize Lucky. I helped her bring him to the vet, say the goodbyes, be a supporter for her and advocate for lessening his pain. I saw Lucky's soul leave his body in a vortex of swirling light (like the most beautiful tornado you ever saw). Within the next thirty minutes, his spirit was running everywhere, so happy to be running and playing. Lucky came to visit me every now and then and a few years after his passing he came with a more serious message. "This is the last time I will see you for awhile. I have a job to do." And he was off.

After my dog, Garcia (a senior, black Cocker Spaniel with the most loving heart), passed away at home, I had a very similar experience. Garcia seemed to come visit and hang around for longer periods of time than Lucky did. However, the day came when Garcia, with his cute floppy ears, came with the same message. I asked him where everyone went when they have jobs, but he said nothing. It was ask if he could not/was not allowed to tell me. During my time of experiencing those who had passed away and meeting spirit guides, I started to come up with my own theory. When someone passed away, they start with a time of being free from the body and discovering that they are immediately full of light and unconditional love. This can last for hours or days. Usually they visit family and friends eager to let them know all is well.

They then pass on to what the Buddhist's call "bardo" and I as a child called "sleep." It is the time when the soul looks at their life. They examine things like what they did and didn't do. What they could have done differently. What good they did and how they may have had pain. For some, it is a "painful" time. I say painful because I think that while we are full of love, we can have a measured disappointment with ourselves. We may have a difficult time accepting what we did, the pain we caused.

Every person's "bardo" takes a different amount of time to go through. A friend of mine whose husband was in his sixties, led a good life, and died of cancer, seemed to pass through it in a month (the shortest I have ever seen). While my father, who had a trying life as an alcoholic and abuser, took about a year. In this time, the soul may feel like they do not want to face these things, but do because it is part of learning. My father abused my mother, and I am told, his first wife as well, while he was intoxicated. The next morning, he had no memory of the occurrences. I suspected my father saw what he did not see in life. It could not be easy looking at the wrongs one created, let alone ones you could not remember creating.

After the "bardo," the soul visits family and friends again, but now with a deeper understanding of life, and holding wisdom and patience in spades. They are like a rock you can lean on, yet they still retain their personality. If Aunty Betty swore like a sailor and laughed endlessly, she would still share those dirty jokes with you. If Uncle Joe was quiet and reserved, Uncle Joe would still be so. Certainly they were all now older and wiser. They could come and go as they pleased. And then the time comes where they may choose to leave your side to do service.

Imagine it as volunteer work in heaven. Time is much different there. I laugh whenever spirit gives me any kind of date range because it is usually so off. They may say "in two months," and suddenly nine months later something occurs. Time is much longer there. To them, time here happens in a blink of an eye. So, when we ask for help or ask for something to happen quickly, and we feel like we are suffering for an eternity waiting, to them only a moment passed (and I am sure they wonder why we are being so impatient!). So, while a loved one's passing may have only happened two years ago, they may have been hanging around for twenty years their time. After awhile, you figure you need something to do, a hobby perhaps. Some may decided to counsel and support those of us on earth, thus becoming spirit guides.

So, here Bob was hanging around for centuries and perhaps he had been a spirit guide before. You know he had been around the block once or twice because of his laid-back attitude and humor. He was like, "Kid, I've seen this all before." And while it took Arabella twenty years to figure out who Bob was, she finally did (and I am sure he was relieved to have the pretenses over with).

That evening, as my head hit the pillow, I felt a cool breeze. How do you tell the difference between air moving around your room and a spirit? The breeze comes to you, very cool, and then stops, hovering in your area. Tired as could be, I could not figure out who was there. I picked up my cell on my nightstand and texted Arabella. "Cool breeze, wonder who is here."

Charlie asked why I was reaching over to my cell and I told him someone was in the room. "What??? Who???" Years ago he asked me to never tell him if anyone was around us, but then he changed his mind.

"Why are you scared? You told me to tell you when it happens," I said.

"I know, but I'm scared of ghosts. Is it a ghost?" he sheepishly asked starting to tuck himself further and further under the covers.

"No. We have no ghosts in this house. Not sure what spirit it is, but no ghost," I replied trying to comfort him.

The next morning, I recalled a significant dream I had during the night. I call them significant when I get big messages or visits from spirit. I was comforting a man in that zen cafe between worlds. He was in his twenties to thirties, had shoulder length black hair, work black clothes, and felt British, but did not have the accent. He was sad he passed away and having difficulty with it. Naturally he was depressed. I mean what a rude awakening it would be to be young and the next moment realized you died. I tried to talk about the wonders of the other side. This fell on deaf ears. So, without thinking, I let all intelligence go. Instead of talking, I let my intuition kick in and I started emanating all the love I could muster from my heart, saw bright white light open from my heart chakra and gave him a hug. I felt myself give him an immense amount of loving, child-like energy, and telling him that it would be OK because now he could help people. I told him how much I loved him and how the love he felt here was a fraction of what was waiting for him on the other side. I woke up after that feeling peaceful. I knew he crossed over.

Later in the day I texted Arabella joking that now "they" are going to put me to work in my sleep. It dawned on me that this was the job that Azrael had in mind— comforting the souls of those who recently died and sending them to the light. It's not like I didn't have enough going on, right? I worked full time, ran a small business and already did energy work and intuitive reading with clients and taught yoga classes. I may not have been on the mountain working for Azrael, but there was work to be done.

After work that day, my daughter and I were catching up on our day when suddenly she said, "There's someone in the room." As I said, "Yes," the cool breeze was back. I told her to hone in on who it was. I could see the outline of this male being, full of light. He moved his face close to hers as they communicated silently back and forth. She said she got a few names, mostly male names. I knew he was telling her who he was, and telling me, thank you for helping him find peace.

CHAPTER 27

Hello God, I Hear You

Before I met Nathan Lane (or God as he is normally addressed), I had not spoken to him, truly spoken with him for years: That, however, was about to change.

The second Friday of every month, I held a Relaxation Yoga class at my studio. This special one and a half-hour class brought the chance to simply melt into a pile of bolsters, pillows and blankets, releasing the week's worth of craziness. During this time, I watched over the students like my flock, guiding them into each station, watching for signs of discomfort, or assisting them with turning to the other side of some asanas. The time between the ringing of the bell (a sound to tell the students to move to the next station) is quiet time for me. I usually spend a few minutes of meditation while the eight to ten minute poses are held.

On this particular Friday evening, the stage was set with music selected by Sara, who visited me while I set up the room. My fellow yogi and meditation instructor stopped by to let me see her in her fabulous purple dress and black stiletto heals. "This is me dressed up. I had to show you. I even put on makeup." While I set up the room, we talked about my long-term goals for my yoga studio. In this moment, Sara noted my Native American woman companion around me said that I was going in the right direction. Before leaving, Sara brought her iPod and told me to play Singh Kaur for my class. I was a little surprised my music choice was changed, but being on a time crunch to complete the set up for class, passively accepted the change as she moved electronics: my iPod Nano out and hers in with music starting to play.

Halfway through class I haphazardly noticed my root chakra was open. It had been blocked for a few months and my lack of paying attention to it was doing no good. After that realization came a steady wave of chi energy that flooded me. My hands, legs, feet, all were filled with energy. Years ago in ignorance, I would think "too much... it's too much," not knowing what it was consciously and trying everything including jumping up and down to get rid of it. In my adult life the past few years, I worked it, enjoying every sensation. It reminds me of when your foot "falls asleep." Some people will let it pass grumpily. Some shake it and try to walk on it. When my chi got high, I now simply felt it and let it move it to areas of the body I needed it. This evening was an unexpected moment of high chi in a time where my mind was distracted with yoga. Instead of my new profound ways of dealing with it, my mind starting going back to the "too much... it's too much." Before I started even contemplating how to jump up and down without disturbing my students, I felt a presence in the room.

Generally, I was able to break up a "presence" into two main initial categories—ghosts and those from the other side, who I refer to as "they." Ghosts generally come through forcefully, very present almost as if I were to have a person standing physically right next to me. "They" usually come through with a softer presence and there is a buffer of sorts between us. Tonight, there was no buffer and so my immediate thought was ghost.

Ghosts scare me. They make my hair stand on end and not in a good way. One minute they are aware they have passed away and the next you are a stranger invading their space and time. Their presence is just unnerving to me, especially without that buffer and oh-so-loving feeling all around. And while tonight's presence did not exhibit the lack of love feeling, my body still thought danger.

This presence did not immediately make themselves known. So, sitting in the meditation space, looking into the room of my flock, I grabbed my cell phone. Now, one would ask the good question of why my cell phone was upstairs when I was teaching yoga. As all things are meant to be and planned for a reason (as my soul sister, Arabella, would remind me that evening). The clock in the yoga studio had decided to work haphazardly a few hours earlier and my cell phone was my clock to know when to tap the singing bowl.

I held my left fingers over the speaker while my right fingers texted, "Feeling chills. Wonder who is here." At that, it was time to ring the bell and move my students to a new station. After everyone was settled and my visitor was not about to leave, I sat on a mat at an open station. Prior to sitting I was drawn to do Reiki on one of the students, and then all of them. Having two new students I thought the idea might be inappropriate to do individual sessions, so I decided to send it to them from afar. As I sat in hero pose, I felt all of this energy pouring out of my hands in every direction, heading to the students and beyond them. I saw above my head white light and then a beautiful woman with long white hair and felt a combination of undefinable love and healing energy coming down from her, through my crown and out my hands. In my mind, I recited a line from the character, Willow, during the final episode of *Buffy the Vampire Slayer*, "Oh, my Goddess," because, that is who she was.

I quickly bowed my head in honor of my students and this being, did the sign of the cross, grabbed my cell phone and headed downstairs as quickly as possible to call Arabella. Meanwhile, the goddess followed me closely.

Arabella picked up the phone and I said, "Goddess." Immediately she said, "yes," and told me I needed to light white candles, that the goddess was asking for white candles. Meanwhile upstairs, I had three white candles burning, one blue and white electronic candles lighting the classroom. The Goddess was not asking, she was telling Arabella the room I had been in.

In our two-minute conversation, she told me to go back upstairs, light the candles and the Goddess wanted to talk to me. She said to be open and not let my thoughts get in the way. However, even if my mind did get in the way, it wouldn't matter because the Goddess will just move them aside and tell you to listen. And she did.

I went upstairs, rang the bell, all the while the goddess instructing me what to do and then, sat on the mat. I went into extended child's pose thinking that it would calm my active mind. She said, "How can you get everything when you are covering your third eye?" I sat up.

She showed me that I, and each person in the room, and each person on the planet were her children. She loved us tremendously. (And let me clarify here, this was not a goddess, this was *the* Goddess.) In my casual nature, I started conversing with her, and complaining, and making excuses for what we talked about next—my writing.

Lately, everyone and their mother seemed to have come out of the woodwork in heaven/the other side, and been stressing the importance of me writing. They all, of course, have their own great ideas about what I should be writing, and to an ADD person, you don't give multiple ideas. So, here I was with the Goddess telling me my life's purpose was to write and I was complaining about it like a two-year-old. She acts like my mother with a firm hand saying there is no getting out of this, no other path to choose, it is what it is. I then started making my demands like my teenage daughter making hers before doing chores. I said, "I need more time in my schedule to write, but need it not to affect my finances." (And then of course started to regret even asking. You never ask for something from spirit unless you have the details to be as specific as possible.) I needed focus and I needed a topic. She told me, as many of my friends, have told me before... just write! She then, seeing my complete lack of ability to make this decision on my own, told me to continue to write about myself.

We discussed my acceptance of being here on earth and my life as it has been this time. I have no regrets in my life. I've always been accepting of it. I realized and yet knew at the same time, it was because my inner knowing saw that it is all there for a reason for the greater good. I then reflected on how sad it is here, how lonely being separated, but I must really enjoy being here because I reincarnate over and over. I apparently could spend an eternity doing service here. I did however start to complain about my next life, not wanting to do it, but that point was also moot and determined.

Years ago I saw my next life. I had always said I want my next life to be a vacation life involving me lying on a chair at a beach sipping a margarita with a hot buff man and not a care in the world. I was told that one had to wait until this next life as a punk teen living on the streets was complete. It would be short and painful. I saw myself in alleyways with dumpsters nearby with other teens. We were part of some anarchist group and the government seemed to be in flux in this country. I had short pink spiked hair and died young.

After class was over and each student had left, I immediately picked up my cell and saw messages from Arabella that were sent before my call to her saying "Goddess."

Her messages said:

"I'm told if you relax and meditate in dark room with two candles you will know. Two white candles... Okay... lol. They are very bossy and specific. Then you will know. Hope you have two white candles. They said white, not ivory. WTF??"

"Why don't they just tell me?? If they can say all that?? Wanna make it hard."

"These peeps stressing me out."

"Trying to talk to me while I'm shopping."

And then after my call to Arabella indicating the visit was from a goddess that by then she also knew, she texted me:

"Lol. When she visits, she is so strong. She is EVERYWHERE! Hair is still standing on end!! P.S. I was right, she is angry about war on women!!! Lol!" (Earlier in the evening before my class, Arabella and I were talking about recent news she saw with women and children being raped. We started talking about the energy moving into a matriarchal society and that might help end that issue, if women would only take the power like Amazonian women did, instead of trying to share the power.)

"But not funny. She scolds me!! Atrocious crimes on women—"

And then Arabella got a name, "Shekinah."

When I called her to touch base on what had happened and how I just read her text messages, she started immediately talking about "Shekinah." She had Googled it, not knowing what it meant, but super excited.

According to the Jewish Encyclopedia, Shekinah is "The majestic presence or manifestation of God which has descended to 'dwell' among men." Wikipedia says, "Like Sofia, Shekinah has sometimes been personified and worshiped as a goddess of wisdom within contemporary pagan religions and New Age spirituality."

The Goddess had even given us her name. And apparently, she had set the stage. Arabella said today she was listening to Chanticleer's "Magnificat a cappella." And as she said in a later text, "Not sure if it is significant, but maybe it is something your holy mother likes." The music, that I had never heard before, and that she was trying to share over her phone at this point, sounded like church music. Tonight I had deeply loving peaceful music set by Sara, a long deeply serene class, a clock that didn't work, a cell phone nearby, a friend in Tampa who was listening to church-like music today and available to talk and receive messages. The other side did indeed have a plan.

What was most surprising was the little message from Arabella at the end of the evening. It was when I asked her who was the Native American lady Sara kept getting that was near me. She said, "You're not gonna want to hear it." She told me that letting go of all preconceptions of religions, and not being afraid to just have the answer be what it was, that the Native American lady, Shekinah, my Shaman male, are all the same—they are God.

This was not hard for me to accept. In my meditation with the Goddess, I asked her that if I say my Hail Mary's would they go to Mary or would they go to her. She said it didn't matter; they could go to either. Then she showed me the construction of the concept of Mary. How, not to say that Mary did not live, but that it is a construct of the human mind for us to break down everything into pieces and how on the other side, everything is one.

Over a year ago in Arabella's lessons from the spirit world, the angel Ariel was showing her the unity of everything. She would see a bird and they would correct her and say, "The spirit of bird." It went on like that—the spirit of dog, the spirit of deer, and the spirit of spider. All connected. Nothing was an individual. And then they showed her "the spirit of man." I found this to be amazing, as it folded in with the Buddhist concept of how when we achieve enlightenment and go back to the source, we fold into all that is. We are no longer individuals. And while I talk to the other side and deal with specific personalities, we are all one community that sings together in song in a choir: no one more special than the other, but no less important, either. All children of the goddess or children of god.

The next day following my encounter with the divine feminine went from feeling cool about the experience to questioning everything. Late Friday evening Arabella said she had more to tell me, but to get sleep and we would talk the following day. Saturday arrived and after a yoga class and a MDT workshop, I called to check in with my dearest friend.

She had said in her text she had two bad things to tell me. I thought perhaps the divine had two things to pass along to her that were not so hot. However, instead I am told, "I did not want to tell you this, so please understand I am the messenger. She told me that I had to tell you."

The night the Goddess visited, I wrote down my encounter. Arabella said before she even read it, she received another message for me. "She said that you need to talk to God."

At first I thought this was going to be like my mother who tells me to eat more despite the fact that I do eat, all day long actually. However, there was more in her voice than just that.

"She said that the Shaman you see is like a grandfather to you. You feel comfortable with him. He is gentle with you. There are no consequences."

Arabella continued, "But with God, there are consequences for our actions and he is more like a father, and you turn away from that. I don't know why you are so scared, but she asked me to tell you to talk to God. Prostrate yourself before him."

She asked what child's pose looked like, the one I mentioned in my writing. When I described to her how extended child's pose is like prostrating yourself before a deity, she started to cry.

"She said that you have turned away from God and he is holding back from you. She said when you were little you had a great relationship with him, but then something changed. You need to go before him like a child again. You need to accept him. Maybe this is why you need to go to church." (During different times in my life I had urges to go to church, which I occasionally fed with a visit to a local Catholic church.)

Arabella wept, as she felt such empathy for the emotions being conveyed. I let her finish. I agreed that the Shaman could be seen as a grandfather. He was neat and interesting, taught me cool things, was patient, and I always felt safe. God on the other hand was authoritarian. I felt safe, but never secure. I felt loved, but there was never love in his voice.

When I was a child, I did have a great relationship with God. I grew up Catholic and went to mass every Sunday. In my teenage years, I sometimes went weekdays before school on my own. During my time in college in New York, I did the readings at church on Sundays. And then something that I cannot put my finger on changed my relationship with God. I was no longer certain there was a God and started to be more interested in was the other side. While I did not challenge whether there was a God or not, I claimed ignorance in saying what there was, I did not know, and who was to say it was a man. The older I got the more the word "God" bothered me. It stuck in my throat like food getting caught, not wanting to go down. The pit of my stomach welled. I felt myself clench up. I had more comfort in words like "Providence" or "Jehovah," but not "God."

And then, shortly after the visit with the Goddess, God made his presence known. I had a dream one evening that I was in a darkened hallway with a door at the end. The door was filled with light. It was God. As he spoke, white and blue light filled the sides of the hallway. I could not remember what words invoked light into one side, but the other was "I am all that is, was and ever shall be." God had spoken and I had listened. Clearly, there was God. You could not wake up from a dream like that and think there was not. This was more than even one of my intuitive dreams. It was real in every sense of the word.

While we spoke, I told her that the message she shared was like your mom telling your sister to tell you that she can't take you and your father not talking anymore, so please be the adult and make up. I was seriously amused by this because I personally would never associate such human emotions with the creator of all life on earth.

"Why would you think that God would not feel those feelings? He is a parent to all of us, you know," said Arabella.

And so my day of going from this super cool moment of talking to "mom" to being scolded that I need to get along with "dad," lead me to do more soul searching. I took time that afternoon to truly open myself up and apologize. I followed the apology with extended child's pose, and then added hands in prayer bowing into the pose.

Later that evening, I decided to have a chat with God. Before doing so, I pulled three cards from "Wisdom of the Hidden Realms," which told me to open up to the divine, go to the well, and go with the flow freely and willingly. And so, I talked again, to God. What did I hear? He wanted me to go to church to show him I care—at least for a little while. He wanted me to "go to the well," which I can only take as meaning opening up to him. He wants me to be spiritual again and spend more time praying.

When you think about it, it really is not asking much. In my day full of work, taking care of my family, running a business and then with some time to eat and sleep, I did not spend that much time deep in prayer. Contemplation? Yes. Meditation? Yes. Feeling the universe around me open to messages? Yes. Talking to God? No.

God didn't need an appointment or a place. He simply needs a moment in time with focus, willingness, and a genuinely open heart.

Talking about God was not easy for me. I become fearful and scared of judgment. It always amazed me how there are so many people that can freely pray, believe and invoke his name. For me, it was a great challenge. Sometimes when I felt spirit was seriously challenging me, I would say, "What more do you want from me? Fine take it. Take it all. I have nothing left to give you." But of course, there was always more to give. In this case, God was challenging me to face one of my greatest fears in life: judgment.

It was almost like being in high school all over again and you are so embarrassed by your parents that you ask them to drop you off to school five blocks away. You never acknowledge you even have parents around your friends. You are so afraid of being ridiculed, of being teased. For me, it would be people thinking I am a Christian radical or crazy.

After that experience, I started to talk to God. I said prayers many evenings before bed, talked about my day and concerns, and sometimes had just random thoughts that I shared. I realized because of Arabella's message that I had pretty much stopped talking to God.

I realized this lesson was one I thought I had worked through. A year before God visited "they" challenged me to talk more freely about being intuitive. It was a huge leap, quite difficult, and like riding a bike. I thought I had nothing left to give and then suddenly, they reminded me, I did. I had to learn that not only do I have a relationship to repair, but I cannot keep it as a secret one. How would your spouse feel if you never brought them out with you or talked about them? What if you never shared pictures of your children?

I had a vision where I saw the silhouette of the holy family against a horizon at sunset. There were purple arrows shooting up to the sky. God showed me he did not create this separation between man and himself. I stood realizing that I created my own separation. And so in my prayers to God, I offered myself fully to do what was best and needed for "thy highest good."

The saying, "Let go and let God," has deep meaning for me after that experience. Instead of asking God for what I needed, instead, I started asking, "What can I do for you today?"

CHAPTER 28

Battle Wounds

I started having vertigo for no reason that I or anyone could associate with an issue. A few months later, I could not bring myself to drive on bridges and highways that rose above ground level. That funneled eventually into a fear of wide spaces while driving, driving fast, and driving on highways. I became limited to back roads on flat ground. Getting anywhere was a struggle. I had seen information on a training for teaching yoga in prisons and told a teacher, Sara, at the studio. I had considered teaching in prisons because of my family's on and off again stints in the penal system. My brother was in and out of jail numerous times for drugs and getting into fights, my dad was jailed for intoxication and spousal abuse until my mother dropped the charges, and my mother was even once in prison. Sara, who had started a non-profit meditation organization was so excited she immediately told me we needed to go.

While I felt I was supposed to be there, I just could not financially swing the fee for the program along with the airfare and hotel need to attend this training in Colorado. However, within a few weeks, Sara said she booked flight and that the meditation organization was going to pay for her and I to attend. I still could not rectify taking time off from work, paying for the training and hotel, and convincing myself it was safe to take a plane. While Sara did not know what I was thinking, my dragging my heels on paying for the training led her to buy my plane tickets, saying that it was to cover the Reiki training I was teaching her.

While she had made the sweetest gesture, I became angry that she jumped the gun. I was having an internal battle about getting on a plane and that someone made a decision for me. I had no choice now but to go. Still uneasy about going, I next was told that the hotel was paid. In the fall of 2012, on the morning we left, still hesitant about going, she even had a driver meet us at the studio to drive us to the hotel.

Sara amused me by giving me time for multiple glasses of wine, which I needed to fly. Before leaving, Kat gave me one of her sacred stones she used to keep her safe. Sara prepared her phone with a meditation for me to listen to upon take off.

The next day, we arrived at a beautiful yoga studio for the Prison Yoga Project training, led by James Fox. We started off talking about what led us to the training. I should have said, *"Well, Sara pretty much dragged me here, paid for everything even though I knew I was suppose to be here."* Instead what came out of my mouth was my family's struggle with the law. It was something I was embarassed about. I was ashamed of my family. And here I was, someone who hardly ever let anyone except for Kat and Arabella get close enough to know me, sharing my deep wounds. Fox led us through yoga classes as he would be teaching one with prisoners. We learned how they too were vunerable. They needed to have a wall to their back. Prisoners needed to know where the exit was. And how, because they had to maintain a mask in prison of being strong, and being in a room with others doing yoga offered them a safe place to open up. As a teacher, you needed to be dedicated and be there. They depended on you as a constant in their lives that brought a semblance of peace to this chaotic place.

He educated us on the prison population and the reality of how many Americans are and have been incarcerated. The statistics were amazing. Most people know someone who has been incarcerated. We talked about PTSD (Post Traumatic Stress Disorder). Many people have heard about PTSD from soldiers coming back from war, but this can occur in anyone who has experienced traumatic events—those who have been raped, abused, seen horrors, survived torture. And according to Fox, many people in the prison system, suffer from PTSD.

I read once that people with PTSD share this fuzziness in memories from when horrible instances happened in our lives. While I have these memories of where I can remember, I also have large gaps of memories. My childhood was colored with trauma. My memory from childhood is like this big black fog. That's all I see sometimes until a memory starts to creep in. When I was younger and the fog started to clear, when I would see a flash of a memory, I moved into hysterical crying fits. I've learned with age to cope. To see those flashes with a distance, as if I am watching another person. But even when something reminds me of a happier childhood memory, it is still cloaked in the pain that colored my early years.

Charlie once told me, "The devil is in the details." Puzzled by what he meant, I asked him to explain. He said, "You can't remember many details of your childhood because that's where evil is, where you experienced it." And he might just be right.

During our intros one woman said for the first ten years of doing yoga, she cried each time she was on the mat. I instantly went back to my days learning Neuro-Linguistic Programming, remembering how trauma is stored in the body. One day during a meeting with friend, he started talking about a painful break-up. While talking about his ex, he started rubbing his shoulder.

"Stan," I asked. "What's wrong with your shoulder?"

He mentioned it was an injury. He believed it was from playing tennis about two years ago.

"When did you break up with your girlfriend?"

"About two years ago. Oh!" he said. That was all he needed to associate the pain in his shoulder with his trauma.

So, if you can imagine that everyone is walking around with these scars that we cannot see. We think everyone is normal, healthy and whole. However, how often do we inquire into the scars of others? We cannot see them like the scrape on the knee or that half-inch scar near a thumb when we cut a little too deep while chopping carrots for dinner. Instead, our scars are buried. We do not see them on ourselves unless we do self-examination. We do not see them on others unless we ask. Our scars make us warriors. We survived individual battles. Instead, we cover them up, hide them, bury them deep inside our subconscious mind and bones and muscles out of shame. Perhaps if we looked at our scars as battle wounds, we might become proud of what we were able to survive through.

The following day, we broke out into groups. Fox advised us to come up with a pitch that we would present to a prison board as to why we should bring yoga into the prison system. As my group was called on, I became the spokesperson. A background with working with sales people became my greatest asset. When other groups went, Fox asked them a few questions or none and moved onto the next group. Fox and I however, went head to head. It was like fast and furious debate. It was personal to me. He kept asking, challenging. I kept answering question after question using stories and data. My heart-pounded and while I was in "the zone," part of me wanted to have a minor heart attack from putting myself out there. At the end of "quiz," the room applauded.

Before we left for the training, Sara took the bull by the proverbial horns and had already met with representatives from the Pennsylvania prison system for us to do yoga in prisons. However, after the training was completed, the prison system declined our offer for free yoga for prisoners.

I came back raw and open, scars exposed from childhood. Sometimes you can fool yourself thinking that you are over something, completely healed. And then you realize, you are not. Forgiving my father when I was thirteen did not make my memories easy to deal with. Even through I felt compassion for my mother, did not make my memories come easier to me. Instead, I realized, these scars are deep, they are scars—always there. However, each day, I can remember I survived and it does become easier to deal with.

God continued his visits, which seemed to happen many times in the bathroom. I know, the bathroom, right? Arabella joked that it was the "throne room." However, if you think about it, it makes sense. When you are in the bathroom, taking a shower, your mind is generally calmer, more open. You are there, not rushing around. Since childhood, the bathroom has been my safe space. And so, it was here in this small room, that I saw myself shrink down into a small child and climb onto God's lap. I sat as he held me. I offered up my innocence, my heart, and my vulnerability. I think that is all he was asking for.

CHAPTER 29

On My Knees

I started off 2013 with kidney stones that left as quickly as they came. A week after that, I was plagued with cold after cold, hitting me systemically. I seemed to follow the pattern of childhood with chronic ear infections and then developing a chronic sinus infection.

I spent the entire month of January crying over anything and everything. If I was sick again, I cried. If I heard or saw something sad, I cried. I cried in my sleep. I cried when I was awake. I cried at home, in the shower, and in the car. I mastered the art of release. For someone who hardly cried prior to this experience, it was a strange time. I went with it. I flowed with my imperfection, and halfway through it, was given the reason for my sadness— the dark side of the moon.

We all have them. Parts of ourselves we don't like. Parts of our personality or life we wish we did not have. I saw them all at once. I started to make peace with my ego, my drive, my temper, my pushiness, my need to be loved. It was the way I was built. Those traits come in handy in many different ways we cannot fathom. I learned to love them. I learned to embrace them. Loving them and acting on them are not one in the same. I could choose to be angry or, I could recognize I was angry, observe it, and let it go.

During the same time I trained with a local yoga school in Vinyasa Yoga. The forty-hour program was spread over multiple weekends. I was a Hatha Yoga girl, but the Vinyasa was a requirement under the school. I pushed my body harder than it had ever been pushed before. One day in class I think we did forty Sun Salutations. My body ached with pain. My muscles stretched into asanas they never could reach before. Students pushed me, pulled me like taffy to open my body up. It was the most emotionally traumatic and physically difficult time of my life, but in the end, I passed my test, knowing the Ashtanga Primary Series in English and Sanskrit and being able to talk someone through it, not needing just my muscle memory to guide the way.

January of the Great Change, Charlie and I decided to close the stores and focus on the wellness studio since that was generating money where the stores were not. My Capricorn hubby was heartbroken. However, shortly after the decision, he was offered a nine to five job doing filming and editing for a credit union. The strain of the years of having the stores, and now closing them, had strained our marriage more so than anything else I could remember. While we spent the first couple of years together and apart for weeks at a time, the past few years was a struggle with seeing one another. Charlie was working a third shift in retail, coming home to sleep and then running the stores. I was working during the day, coming home for a catnap and then at the studio. He was a night owl. I was a morning person. We were always working with little time to see one another. When we did, we managed to bicker, as I did not like the way he ran the stores and he didn't think it was fair for me to criticize while he was there daily. As the days warmed, and when I was healthy, I spent my time outside alone more and more.

The year so far had been challenging with decisions to expand the wellness studio and subsequently months later, looking to downsize. Practitioners at the studio came and went. I became the one steady constant, and I was sick—all the time.

In the spring, I went to New Jersey for a Thai Yoga Massage training. We would all take turns being guinea pigs during lessons for the teacher and each other. From my recent Vinyasa training, I was pliable and the Floridian instructor was able to fold me completely over my legs. I had never been able to lay my chest on my legs before in Paschimottanasana.

By May, I had been sick over twenty-five times and stopped counting. What was my body telling me? An ENT doctor finally helped me in discovering my sinus passage and nose had been having major problems which was causing my chronic infections. I started to slow my schedule down. I gave myself off on Sundays. More and more, I allowed myself to sit on my back porch or lay on my couch watching a movie, not working. This was not easy at first. My mind went back to "how do people relax?" My body was exhausted. My emotions were spent. I needed to run away.

Everyone's life around me was changing, but I felt frozen in fear and illness. I asked Charlie one day, "When is my big change going to happen?" What I didn't know was that I was about to stumble right into it.

CHAPTER 30

Through the Belly of a Whale

The summer of 2013, I saw on the community bulletin board at work, flyers for Central PA Holistic Conference. I hadn't been to the conference in almost ten years and while I had considered going the past couple of years, the timing was always off, as that was the weekend I always took my daughter to her summer camp.

Charlie offered to drive Hope to her summer program so I could attend. He knew how important it had become to me to start to mingle with my tribe. I had become completely about work. I rarely saw my friends. While I had this beautiful wellness studio where people came to me, I felt like I was always working.

In the workshop room, I gazed around, looking for familiar faces. I saw Phoenix, who came over to say hello. It was strange at first to see this man I once loved and his sweet mother nearby. I had heard a few years ago he had a son. We talked about him and about my daughter.

I found a seat where I put my blanket, drum and eye pillow for our shamanic journey. An anthropologist/shaman from California was leading the weekend's headline workshop. Journeys are like guided meditation without so much words being spoken, but rather we know where we will go and take a trip to the space between here and the other side, receiving messages, connecting with those who've past, and more. During these journeys, we were given a mission while the teacher drummed.

On the first journey, we went to our "garden," a place in our mind that would be relaxing. I don't know if we were going to a building nearby, but my mind instantly went to a place I previously went to in a Yoga Nidra. I climbed spiral stairs up through the clouds until I arrived in a courtyard with raised garden beds and koi fishponds. My temple was in front of me. In my Yoga Nidra journey, the temple doors were closed. I ran to a safe guarded by a monk and never got to the safe. Here, the temple doors were wide open and I again ran to the safe, finding it unprotected. The safe was open. Lying on the floor beside it was a human heart in a puddle of blood.

I ran out of the temple into the courtyard hysterically crying, longing, sad. I could not stop the tears, could not breathe. My spirit animals surrounded me—eagle, wolf, bear, raven, and pushed me into the water. I came up for air, crying hysterically only to once again dunk me back in. Over and over this happened until I could rise from the water without crying. I then went for a swim.

There was no life in this pond and it connected endlessly to everything around it. No water lilies, no plants, no fish, just murky green tinted water contained in a seemingly concrete narrow structure. I swam and swam.

The morning of my journey, I awoke with the sign of Neptune in astrology in my mind. Neptune was the son of Saturn who swallowed all of his children to prevent them from usurping his power. Neptune sat in his father's belly contemplating. He learned about life, death and resurrection. He learned intuition and emotion. Like Neptune, I saw a whale nearby and swam into its mouth, resting in its belly. I sat like Neptune until I felt myself slowly piece my emotions back together. When I was ready to leave, I could not exit through the mouth. I tried over and over again. I did not want to pass from the bowels, but eventually I knew that was the way out. Gross right? It wasn't that I did not want to pass that way because of the nature of it, but more that I wanted to come back the way I started. I knew there was no way to do that. I had to pass just like our body rids things that are not good for us.

And so I passed and swam into the ocean, saw my water dragon I've dreamed of several times. Instead of being afraid, I passed by my friend with a "hello." I went back to the temple, back to the safe. The safe was open, but now there was a ball of pink light inside. Pink light is associated with the high heart (unconditional love). My journey was over.

As I cried during my journey, I was grateful to have the eye pillow to cover my face and wipe my tears. All I could think about was how the people here would think I was completely loony crying after a mere shamanic journey.

My heart ached. I longed like there was nothing else around: intense, unstable, all emotions rising to the surface, suffocating longing. I could not explain where this was coming from and why. Where there at once was tapered, conscious emotion (and of course, sometimes not conscious), now there was everything without thought. Thought could not hide it, could not quiet it, could not put it in a box and contain it. My heart chakra opened wide.

In the movie, *I.Q.*, Meg Ryan is engaged to a scientist. Her car breaks down and she meets this mechanic. Instantly spark after spark flies. Her uncle, the aged Einstein and his two comical sidekicks, all engage in creating opportunities for Meg Ryan to get out of her head and into her heart—where Tim Robbins (the mechanic) is. She fights and fights this with every fabric of who she was. Until one day, she opened up.

I imagined my council of elders, those that have passed that watch over me, trying to create moments over and over again in my life where they tried to engage my heart. A ping here, a nudge there. *"She is too much in her mind,"* they would say. Patiently trying again and again. Until one day, when they were discussing what to do next, they watched my heart blow wide open.

I asked myself, *"How does everyone walk around feeling like this?"* I already feel what people are feeling. I feel their thoughts. I feel their pain, their anguish, their joy, concern, judgment—how could I possibly function at this state? But this love emanating, these feelings of fear, doubt, anger, sadness, longing, are all contained inside me, reflecting back to me.

I was sure they were throwing a party up there on the other side. I wished there would have been a forewarning so I could have prepared. But really, had I known, would I have allowed myself?

Over the past year, I have undergone so many growth lessons and changes. A detachment to the thought that you have to only be good and pure and hide all of those other irritating emotions under the rug. I've learned you don't have to use them, but they are there for a reason. I've learned to start nurturing myself, providing myself with the gift of time. In all of these shifts and changes, everyone I have visited/consulted for energy work or chiropractic care, tells me two things: 1) Your heart chakra is closed, 2) What are you so afraid of?

I had not known my heart was closed. I did not know I was afraid. My cycle as a soul is that I am ever peeling back the layers of the onion, which when I think I've got it, spirit laughs and says, "OK dear one, here is another." I find there was another thing to release, another thing I was afraid of, another level to my growth as a person. And I am fine with that. I love it in *Little Women* when Frederick says, "We are all hopelessly flawed.""

No one is perfect. We are all ever-evolving beings. There is no shame in feeling pain, sadness, moving through change. And yet, we see this deep need to put a mask on.

A month before the conference, I attended Kundalini Tantric Numerology workshop. We did a few hours of Kundalini Yoga, followed by finding our numbers. My challenges and strengths in this life were so clear it was if someone had taken all of the information my soul knew about itself and laid it on paper in front of me.

My Soul Challenge: I am a shaman, but I am challenged with connecting to my soul (higher self) and have a hard time believing I can create the reality that I want. My Karma Challenge: I have a difficult time denying others, even if it pains me. I project happiness all the time, to avoid showing how I feel because I am afraid what others will think of me.

My Gift: a meditative mind with the ability to balance (thought and emotion), a counselor and someone who is able to read between the lines and meet people where they are, long term thought and can access the akashic records (the information of what our live has been through any lifetime and in this life). My Destiny: Teacher, leader, deep knowledge with innate knowledge from past lives. Ability to teach, good with children, lots of energy. I learn through the body. Half man, half God—balanced. And my Path Number (What I wish for myself/what I need to obtain for overall fulfillment): Desire to know that I can communicate all I know. I am the recorder. I need to know the big picture of life.

When doing my numbers I asked my teacher about a pattern I saw. All my numbers in each section added up to my path number—9. She smiled, got excited and said, "That's in the next workshop."

As I move through this journey, I know there will be another and another. Spirit told me this past year that I "have been Fire and Air. Now Tree and Water. At the end I will be Earth."

I went back for the afternoon workshop. Our journey entailed meeting with our "council of elders" (those that help us with our life's plan). In a garden with a picnic table in the middle, was a group of men all dressed up in various robes of color, arguing and laughing about what to do with me. I asked where the women were and suddenly a woman appeared. She said there were a couple of them for me, but they only come out when the men are misbehaving or being too relaxed. They come to clean up the mess was the gist of her message.

On the table was a contract—my life contract. I looked at it trying to read the words. All I could read was a yellow post it note stapled to it. The note said, "The New Book." I lifted it up and under on my contract was written, "The Book." I took it to mean what I was writing. I didn't want to write a new book. I wanted my book! I grabbed the post-it note, ripping it off, and ran as fast as I could. Later Arabella laughed, saying that it had nothing to do with the book. I just changed my contract.

I always found such comfort in children and animals. You can be yourself with them and they will still love you unconditionally. So, mini Phoenix and I played many games of tag after our journeys were complete. We were silly together and made what little conversation one could have with a five-year-old happen. The next day, at the closing ceremony, we sang a few songs like Rainbow

Connection, the conference's annual classic. Phoenix's son told me, "I remember you. In my brain."

"I remember you, too," I commented.

After a few moments of hard thinking, he said, "That's stupid!"

Phoenix who was nearby and heard the conversation and jumped in. "No, that's not stupid. Sometimes we remember things." Phoenix then explained how he thought his son was the reincarnation of his father who passed away about two years after we broke up. If his son were the reincarnation of his father, that would explain how he would remember me.

Since the conference, I hardly slept, rarely ate, was in a state of shock from my emotions, and my heart was doing this weird thing. I finally realized that the wave of electricity pulsing and shocking my heart, extending out to my fingers, was my heart chakra opening. It felt like paddles to the heart bringing me painfully back to life. Wouldn't everyone be delighted!

I told Charlie I didn't know if I wanted to be married to him anymore. Every day we hashed this out: him crying, being angry, being confused as to where this came from. How would my daughter forgive me? How would I ever forgive myself? What if I was making the biggest mistake of my life?

Over the almost eight years of our marriage, I asked, seduced, coerced, cried and begged for physical affection. Charlie could not give me any of those things. He suffered from depression. He was on antidepressants since we met. The drugs kept his emotions tightly closed, only to open into a river of depression every so often.

I knew he loved me. He would cut off his arm for me. Every now and then he would listen and after a few weeks, fall back into his isolation pattern. He would spend evenings by himself working on projects around the house, playing video games or watching movies. We saw each other for a few minutes every evening when he would give me a list of things I needed to do around the house or outside, tell me a monologue about his day, a movie or something he read online, and then he was back to being by himself.

While I too was an introvert, I did need some time around people. Years of being alone had turned me into a female version of everything I didn't like about Charlie: emotionally repressed and isolated.

Was I the Zen Reiki practicing, psychic Susan during this time? No. Was I the yoga abiding Susan following the ahimsa "Do no harm?" No. I was a broken human being. I never promised to be perfect. I only hoped to be good. And in this case, I was not.

When you don't know your own mind anymore, when you don't know your own heart and you haven't been sleeping or eating and have been working crazy hours because people at your work are also sick, you just fall apart.

Another visitor entered my world. At first I could not identify who it was, but it seemed to be present with me in the car, in my room, while I was writing. The one clue I was getting was that I had bursts of creativity run through me when this energy was around.

One day in the car, I heard a story on NPR of artists referring to the concept of creativity as a being. At that moment, something clicked and my mind rushed once again with words to write, projects to work on. I introduced myself with a big thank you for this being entering into my life once again. I had been moving through life for the past few years focusing on the left-brain that my creative side was starving. It ached to be fed, nourished and played with. However, I had to make a request to "The Spirit of Creativity," as I now called her, that when I was not able to write all of the inspiration she was giving me, would she kindly hold onto it for later. I would invite her back and ask humbly that she remind me then. I also decided to use my voice recorder app on my phone for those moments when I was driving and she would get overly excited.

Archangel Jophiel and Gabriel both entered the scene again. Both angels helped people with communication and when it was time for me to get creative, it felt like a party. However, I was still dealing with all of my emotional issues at the same time. I needed to start becoming whole again.

I started slowly nurturing myself back to health. I wrote in a diary. I fed myself. I gave myself breaks. I allowed myself creative time a few hours a day. I put myself to bed early.

Charlie asked me to see a couple's therapist with him. I felt I owed him that. I owed our marriage that. I made a promise to him almost eight years ago and I was breaking it a little more each day. At the therapist's office, Charlie said how he thought I was being dramatic and exaggerating my needs and how he thought everything was fine. He didn't want to lose me. I told them both that I was mentally checked out of the marriage unless someone wanted to convince me I was going through a mid-life crisis or this was normal. Our therapist asked we hang out together doing small and large activities reaffirm each other daily and find the love we once had for one another.

"No. I can't do that. I said I would come here and I have. I can reaffirm him daily because he is a beautiful person, but I can't go backwards. I can't find that love right now."

What I didn't say was how on Saturday morning I crawled out of bed to go teach my morning yoga class and when I looked at Charlie, I felt a spark of love. I was scared. I could not go through another ten years living this way though. I couldn't love someone who couldn't love me the way I needed to be loved. My astrological chart said that what I didn't resolve now would be repeated in fourteen years and be more difficult. I didn't want to go through this again.

When I was a teenager I saw a vision of myself as an old woman. In my twenties, I saw another one. I was alone, traveling, and was full of joy. Whether the person I was with was not in that picture or I was alone, I don't know. I used to think it meant I was going to be alone as an old woman, but full of joy nonetheless.

As Charlie and I started to read our homework assignment together and going to therapy on our own, my thoughts on relationships changed. I fell in love in an instant, but not because of hormones or because I find a person to be a good partner. I fell in love because of the soul experience I had with someone in a past life or a vision of a future. I fell in love with the memory or dream. I, like many, fell in love with a dream. I was not in the present moment in a relationship. This was the one place where my intuition, my connection to the other side was a hindrance.

While my intuition could be used to know when Charlie was upset or where his migraine was stemming from, it hampered my ability to love him unconditionally without worrying about where we "came from" and where we were going. Sometimes you just don't have all the answers. For someone who likes to read the end of a book before starting it, I realized I was doing the same thing in relationships. What I realized is that there is no forever. Whether it is death or something that changes a relationship, you and your loved one will always have a finite time together. So, if you find that person, that treats you well, and you know you have this gut-wrenching need to be with them, you should. It's scary not knowing if it is forever or how long it will last. The time spent together though, that's what makes it magical.

Relationships are two people coming together to build a life together. As we did our work together, I found my Taurus rising, creeping up once again calling for discipline. Balance seems to be the key here. Learning to balance my intuition with the present moment. Learning to balance my need for adventure and my need for taking care of day-to-day things. Learning to balance my love for Charlie, his good points, while balancing the things I needed.

I spent too many years in relationships with people who were not good for me. It didn't mean they were not good people. We were not a good match. I wanted to know the ending and they wanted to be in the middle of it. We both wanted different things from life. Finding a partner is more than finding a soul mate. There's a practicality to it. Do they want what you want? Do you have things in common? Can you also still stand apart from one another and be happy, as well?

Charlie could not read my mind. Charlie was stuck in his own mind, as well. We needed to meet somewhere in the middle and realize that we still both wanted the same things, but needed to bend a little for each other. Relationships are compromise.

I grew up in so many different places, staying in one location was difficult for me. I would begin to fidget, change furniture, and then needed to do something different to compensate. Charlie grew up in only two homes his whole life, where not much was moved, but rather grew from what was there. For him, change was scary. Change a painting on our wall, and that would open up an argument. However, once we realized that he needed the painting to stay and why, and I needed the painting to change, and why, we could start to negotiate needs.

CHAPTER 31

Om

By October, Charlie and I made the decision to stay together. I had realized that 1) if I needed to work my issues out, I'd rather work on them with Charlie, than anyone else. 2) He loved me unconditionally. How often do you meet someone that loves you unconditionally? Crooked nose, morning breath, temper tantrums, snoring. No matter what it is, that person knows you and loves you anyway. 3) I did love Charlie. I just forgot. And to me, that was part of taking the next step with him—to be afraid of what I could feel, the vulnerability, and yet, still take the plunge into loving him. Sometimes you just have to love what's good for you.

It wasn't easy of course. We continued going to therapy on our own. We spent many evenings communicating our feelings, no matter how uncomfortable it was for either of us. Hal Hartman's *Finding the Love You Want* was a daily reading. Plus, we made more time to spend with one another and learned to adjust our learned behaviors to ones that were more conducive to making us both happy.

We also received help from Archangel Chamuel. In August, I started having a visitor who was making his presence known, but I could not figure out who this visitor was. I called Arabella who was able to quickly tune into his name. I looked him up as soon as we got off the phone. As always, I laughed at how Arabella could just pull these odd angelic names out of thin air. I discovered that Chamuel helped people strengthen relationships. He told me after meditation with him one day that by October it would all be decided.

Charlie also made a huge decision. He stopped his antidepressants. He had been on them since he was a teenager. Coming off of this type of medicine is not something that is taken lightly. Many doctors would disagree. However, if one of the problems was his emotional detachment, he wanted to try. About a month into it, not knowing what he had done, I told him how happy he had seemed lately. That was all he needed. He told me about his decision.

What we could not have guessed was that Charlie was a whole other person off his meds, but not the way most people would think. My mother needed to be on medication to stop her manic behavior. Charlie was engaged, affectionate, and laughed! He was a funny guy, this I had always known. But to see him smiling and laughing for more than mere moments was rare. Instead he was serious, all about getting things done. Now he was that person I met, which sounds weird. However, when you fall in love, your body pumps all of these natural chemicals causing you to be happy, joyous, your best self. Charlie was now more like when we first were together. He wasn't too busy to hug me. Hugs were real now, not just a one second encounter with a pat on the back. He was affectionate. He was fulfilling my needs. I had to also bend to fulfill his needs, too.

I had to learn that when he did chores around the house, that was more than chores. That was the way he expressed his love. I grew up where gifts meant I love you. Charlie grew up where you built something, drew a picture, or cleaned a room to express that love. We didn't understand each other's means of expressing love. We started to understand. So, when Charlie really needed me to do laundry, I needed to do it. Putting it off would mean I didn't love him. And he learned that flowers and books every now and then, were well received by me.

He actually became much better at gift giving. I remember him telling me that his father had the worst luck with buying gifts for his mom (i.e. a moose head one year). Charlie equally had the worst luck with gifts. One birthday, I bought myself an agnihotra fire kit like Angel had. Charlie bought me cow dung from a local farmer for it. It wasn't dried or the correct size pellets I needed. He wrapped it up in newspaper. When we went through moments like this, I felt like he didn't know me.

For all of the arguments and fearing when holidays came around, we started to slowly get better at gifts. Actually, Charlie started to be much better, getting me what I would ask for instead of what he thought I needed. I on the other hand started to lose my magic touch with gift giving, which he laughed at saying, "That's OK. You have years until you catch up with me."

How Often Do You Get to Cook for Monks?

In October, we received a visit at our studio from Ven. Peradeniya (Bhante) Sujatha, a Theravada Buddhist monk from Woodstock, Illinois. Bhante, as he is known, had been visiting our area about two times per year and started a bit of a buzz about his visits. He often visited area churches, community centers and yoga and wellness studios.

We were blessed to have him join us at Barefoot for an evening talk on meditation. Bhante's tour was meant to raise money for his monestary, Blue Lotus Buddhist Temple & Meditation Center, however, he did not charge a fee for his talk. He only accepted donations and believed that what was needed would come. Talk about faith!

We filled our classroom with those who knew Bhante from previous visits and newcomers. When Bhante arrived, this petite man filled the space with a balanced quiet determination and humbleness. As soon as he spoke, the room filled with his energy—kindness, humor, and compassion. Anyone around this monk would feel his calm presence and couldn't help laughing with him. Doning burgundy robes and seated on a zafu cushion, Bhante brought buddhism, meditation, and living life down to the most basic concepts. He made it simple. He explained how we, as Westerners, have so many choices. In simpler lives and countries, the people may prepare tea, and only have one kind to make. If you want tea, you have tea. However, here, when we want tea, we have to think about which one we were craving. Was it English Breakfast or Calming tea today? How about a tea with some mango flavoring or perhaps we needed a Yerba Mate for energy? With so many choices, we become anxious. He made you feel like at the end of the day, life can be easy. You just need to meditate.

In another story he talked about how the monestary is in a former church. He kept a cross up so that Christians who wanted to learn about meditation, could come and feel comfortable. In turn he felt like he was doing his life work, helping people. Bhante made Buddhism digestable for non-Buddhist westerners.

This evening was my daughter's first experience with a buddhist monk. She fell in love with Bhante instantly and was glued to his every word as she herself sat on a meditation cushion instead of a chair. After the talk, she, along with others, reviewed the wares his assistant brought. Each piece sold provided money for his monestary and their outreach programs. Hope's pick (since she got her learners permit that year) was his cd, *Driving with Bhante.*

Most people group Buddhist monks together, but much like Christianity, Buddhism has its different veins. His Holiness the Dalai Lama is Tibetan Buddhist, which is Mahayana Buddhism, to which most people are accustomed. Bhante was Theravada Buddhist, which is practiced by almost two-thirds of people from his home country of Sri Lanka. Like Christianity, most Buddhist religions have more in common than not. The most apparent difference between Mahayana and Theravada that I could see was in the form of meditation. Mahayana Buddhism, influenced by Hinduism due to its evolution, uses many visual applications in their practice. Theravada, the oldest surviving form of Buddhism, focuses on the breath in meditation.

Just a mere few weeks before Bhante's visit, I had a call from a gentleman out of the blue who wanted to bring a group of Tibetan Buddhist monks to Barefoot for several days. I missed out on the opportunity the previous year, as I did not have enough interest to warrant hosting a group of monks. After all, this was how they made their living. Just like how in certain Asian countries monks will start the day by bringing their bowl down to the villagers for food in exchange for a blessing, these monks raised money for their monestary in India. Their sacrifice of one year away from their home, traveling from town to town in a cramped minivan, was the way to send money home for food and other basic necessities.

However, now I was renewed with invigoration to bring them in. There was a reason I was getting this call.

One month after Bhante's talk, the Gaden Shartse Tibetan Buddhist Monk tour visited for four days. Charlie and I spent time making meals for the monks, and altering space to accommodate various events from a personal healing session to a group healing to a workshop. For three days, we were go, go, go.

The evening they arrived at their lodging, the tour organizer and the Lama greeted me with the traditional white scarf blessing. I prepared their meal in the kitchen that evening where I witnessed a group of monks pray in Tibetan over the food, eat quickly, and disappear for an early night after a long car ride.

The next day, the monks did a tea ceremony for me, blessing Barefoot. It was a beautiful gift from them, one that I did not ask for, but happily accepted. There was no time in this space as the monks and I sat on zafus while they chanted the sacred words of blessing in deep unison gutteral sounds. I could hear the choir of angels I heard on occasion at Barefoot start to sing in accompaniment. Soon the room echoed with monks and angels, both with their own beautiful songs, complimenting each other.

Throughout the next few days, I received a yarn necklace blessed with one thousand prayers during the Vajravidharan Healing Ritual and during the Empowerment on the Buddha Maitreya. The organizer gave me a seed to chew filled with ten thousand prayers.

"How does this happen?" Charlie asked, after receiving his own yarn necklace.

"Back at the monestary, each day, the monks who are sitting together meditating and chanting have to blow a prayer into different objects. We do this for several hours each day," said one of the English speaking monks who acted as the translater for the Lama.

I watched each healing session performed with such tradition and ritual. During my personal Vajravidharan Healing Ritual, I underwent purification, which involved tea being poured over the top of my head and into a bowl and a piece of dough that also went into the bowl after I released what I needed to by blowing it into the dough. The bell was rung. Incense was burned in my small office. I felt blessed. Some participants came out crying from all of the releasing they were doing.

I had selected as part of my schedule to hold an Empowerment on the Buddha Maitreya, the Buddha of Boundless Love, because frankly, we all need love in our lives. What I did not know, as we all sat together in this classroom in Central Pennsylvania, was that we together were committing to reincarnate in two thousand five hundred years when it was believed the Buddha Maitreya would reincarnate again. I felt connected to every soul in the room. All I could think of was *Wow, in 2,500 years, I will once again see this Lama again. I will see Charlie and Hope again. Every person in this room is now connected. I wonder if we will remember one another.* And what I wanted to say to everyone was *See you in 2,500 years!* It felt like a moment from the film *Cloud Atlas*.

As part of the ceremony, their sculptor had spent the day making a butter sculpture to represent the Buddha Maitreya. Each of us had this "cake" touched upon our heads, reaffirming its love.

The final day of the monk tour was filled with an abundance of giving. We started off the morning with a Che Drol Healing and Purification. During this ceremony, we are given an image of the Diety Green Tara and yarn was wrapped around us, binding us to one another, and then ceremonially cut. The cutting of the yarn represented removing the negativity in our lives and then we were blessed with protection.

After the Che Drol, the Lama presented me with gifts for myself, my husband and daughter, reminding me of my mother's family who upon seeing each other, give gifts. For my family it could be anything from alcohol to clothes to jewelry to perfume. With the monks it was jewelry, incense, mala beads, clothes, and of course, the customary white scarf and blessing.

However, before they departed, as another gift for hosting them, the Lama and his translator gave me a

Tibetan astrological chart reading. My reading was somewhat familiar and somewhat surprising.

"Your health and wealth is OK. Sometimes you have friction with your relatives. You can have negative impact from others who think bad thoughts about you. You will have seven major problems your whole life. You put lots of effort into your work. You seek others advice and rarely make your own decision. In a past life you were a Coo Coo bird. You have a sharp mind, very smart, but cannot use it to achieve all your goals. You may have two different homes, one here and one there. Even though you didn't receive love from your parents, you are doing very well. You will be a bird or gull in next life. You help others and do positive action, but their (the people I help) responses are not good—not in the same manner as you are."

By now, I was reeling. The Lama spoke no English. The translator only some. I hadn't shared a word of my family or my feelings, aside from gratefulness for them being there. And this reading was a one way dialogue.

The Lama verified birthmarks on my body (ones he could not see during our exchanges over the past few days). He confirmed what I always felt, but so many denied me of, the acknowledgement that I deeply feel the emotions of others and that it affects me. And that I know when people feel or say negative things about me. Those thoughts, as I told Charlie many times, they just hang out there like gray clouds that won't go away! When someone has a passing negative thought, that sucker hovers in the air for upwards of five or more minutes. Thoughts are not just thoughts in your head. They are real forms of energy. Ever wonder why just being around someone negative makes you feel sad, angry or depressed? Or perhaps you even feel like certain people are sucking you dry? It's because it's really happening to you. We can't all be perfect all the time, but the more mindful we become, certainly the happier and content we are. Plus, we become more mindful of our own thoughts, which helps everyone.

When I shared the content of my reading later, Charlie right away pointed out my two homes.

"You have one foot in each world," he said reminding me of my favorite description a few psychics told me on separate occasions.

"You are a bridge." I am a bridge between this world and the other side, one foot in both worlds.

My other "aha" moment from my reading came much later. The gull thing. In Buddhism if you reincarnate as an animal, you are on essentially a rocky spiritual path. I did not feel that was true and had such a fit for weeks after the reading about my lack of spiritual progress. However, slowly I came to terms of how when I was young (and even still now), I would have so many dreams about flying! It made more and more sense I must have had a life as a bird. And what was the real kicker was how I had been telling spirit for many, many years that I wanted my next life to be a vacation life. I had suffered enough in this one. I wanted to be on a beach, drinking a margarita without a care in the world. Now, as long as I did not reincarnate as a seagull who lives in a Walmart shopping center (you know what I'm talking about), I think it was a big laugh on the part of spirit to say, "Well, you didn't specify what species you would be on that beach!" Remember, always be specific with spirit.

I recall one evening years ago when my daughter had a crush on a schoolmate. She said she wanted to be in a relationship with him. She wrote it on a piece of paper and burned it in our fireplace like she had seen me do many times before. The following day in English class, when reading Shakespeare's *Romeo and Juliet,* can you guess who was Romeo and who was Juliet? Be very specific. They have fun up there. And besides, the world doesn't interpret our thoughts we want to manifest. It just does it.

We said our goodbyes with a final photo, in which Charlie fulfilled one of my dreams. He brought our dogs to the studio so that my Shih Tzu, could see the monks. I know... silly. However, since I found my rescue, the Shih Tzu, I knew he was a Lama in many past lives, I was certain. And to prove my point, I would show Charlie and Hope how he would suddenly become calm when I played the singing bowl or attempted deep chanting like monks. In this life, he was starting his cycle all over again to learn new things. Of course, he's a dog and just acted with the monks like he did with every person. He wanted to jump on them, calling them his new best friend.

Charlie who loves to cook, said as the monks left, how he felt blessed to provide food all weekend as an act of service. "I mean, how often do you get to cook for a group of monks!"

CHAPTER 32

Ahimsa

The year of the black snake kicked my rear end. I was born in the year of the fire dragon. And while dragons are in the same reptilian family, they show no mercy to one another apparently.

However, the year was ending well. Aside from the visit from the monks, my life had another big moment—I started another yoga training. This time, I was getting my (yes, official folks) 200 hour registered yoga teacher training. I decided to bury my rebellious nature and irritation with Yoga Alliance for their strict protocol. To me, holistic arts was something that you learned, but you can't learn about Reiki in a massage school no more than you could get certified in yoga from a school. Yoga was a time honored tradition of a student studying under a teacher, his/her guru, until at such time the guru says the student is ready to teach. This institutionalizing of an ancient art was not my scene. However, sometimes you need to pick your battles and I decided I might as well hold my energy for one that I might win.

I studied with a woman a few years younger than me in a room filled with around twenty yoginis and one yogi. I felt immediately welcomed, challenged with various asanas, but with patience. This teacher was wiser in her youth than so many teachers I had met. We learned, among many things, philosophy, studying the yoga sutras and the yamas and niyamas (essentially like a Christians ten commandments of what to do, but then adding additional steps on how to be with God). Plus we spent time chanting various mantras including "Om," my favorite sound. "Om" is said to be the sound that created the universe, the sound of God. I celebrated my thirty-seventh birthday at my favorite greek restaurant. When I lived in Astoria, I was blessed to have access to not only my Greek landlord/surrogate grandmother, but lots of Greek restaurants around me. I grew up on feta cheese. I had missed having access to those Mediterranean flavors. Here, a new restaurant had opened the previous year. I even invited friends.

This birthday was the first in seven years where I did not fear getting older, running from my age like it was an infection. We ate great food, enjoyed each other's company and just plain caught up on each other's lives. I mean how cool is it to celebrate a birthday with people you love who are talking about babies growing and making kundalini yoga sounds all in one place. It was my perfect life, a blend of smiles and love with everyday moments and served with a side dish of New Age stories.

I ordered a tray of desserts for us to share and much to my happy embarrassment, the servers sang happy birthday, along with my friends and a nearby table of patrons. My ego instantly made the wish for no more birthday songs to be sung to me as I blew out the candle. I was way too shy for that. However, then I took it back. No matter how embarrassing it was, I was blessed to have people to sing to me and humbled to have another year to celebrate.

CHAPTER 33

All You Need is Love

About two years ago, my friend and teacher, David, held an attunement for Seraphina Rose. This was part of a series of energy attunements with the angels, each with a specific energy. Seraphina Rose is unconditional love. Like all energy attunements, there is a practice of how to give the attunement; this was different with its long prayer-like words bringing in the energy.

As I sat there receiving the energy, I felt it slowly work its way around me until finally it settled in my heart. I felt a deep peace burrow in there, cradled by an enormous love. When providing Reiki for someone who needed it, I would call on Seraphina Rose to share this with the person I was working on. What I had not expected was that every time I offered this up, I also felt this deep love.

In a book I had been reading, *Daughter of Fire*, by Irina Tweedie, in her fifties, she seeks, longs for, and studies under a Sufi in India. Ultimately she is seeking a connection to everything. What she learns is love. This Sufi's tradition is to completely break down who you are and replant love. When love fills the heart, you are connected to God. Irina starts to feel herself break down like a lover in unrest with the Sufi. Tears, anger, longing, sadness and doubt—it creeps up on her slowly, coming and going in waves. In this tradition, loving the Sufi is loving God. He provides a means of connection.

We are all seeking, longing for that connection with someone, sometimes so much so it can be overwhelming— the need for love. We believe we love God (for those that do believe in God), but that is not enough. So, we roam through our daily lives looking for it from others.

When we are born, we hopefully receive it from our parents or those who raised us. We then look for it from partners, sometimes friends. My friend Arabella surprised me one day early in our friendship over fifteen years ago when she said to me, "I love ya." It was such a surprise to hear those words from a friend. You usually reserve that for family (whether you mean it or not!) or a partner. I eased slowly into accepting this. Not that I didn't know that she loved me, but to hear her say it, was strange. She was my friend. Slowly, I started saying back "I love ya."

I spent the next several years practicing that on friends I would meet—"I love ya." For some reason the "ya" made it seem less intense, easier to accept. Perhaps the "ya" identified a casualness that was not as threatening. At first I used it to be a less intense form for me. I found that it eventually tapered the confusion of friends to hear.

As uncomfortable as I was hearing that at first, I saw the look in the eyes of friends as I said it. I heard the hesitation on the phone of "what do I do with that?" Sometimes they came around and said it back. Other times they did not, but I knew they still loved me. And every now and then, when I was around people who were more comfortable with love in many different shapes, did they say it willingly and meaningfully, and usually without the "ya."

In Deepak Chopra's book *The Path to Love,* he cites a list of what love is supposed to accomplish, which includes making us safe, feeling renewed, bring us peace and bring us closer to God. Chopra is not referring to any of these as things we should seek from a partner. These are things that are available to us from ourselves, if we let ourselves have them in our lives. Just as in Irina's experience of feeling love through the Sufi to connect with God, these truths are for us to have with ourselves, our higher consciousness which ultimately is our relationship with God.

However, no matter how in tune I was with my intuition, I am at the end of the day, a human being. I have blind moments like everyone else and that included being blind with love.

When my daughter was little she would get endlessly frustrated that she couldn't tie her shoes by a certain age and couldn't whistle. I told her that, "everything happens in its own time. You have your own pace."

And like her, I have my own timing. When I am ready, it will happen. It doesn't mean immediately. I may not get it until the fifteenth time I try something. However, in my own time, it will happen. One day, I will truly understand that loving myself, loving the God in me, is enough. I have many choices. I am on a spiritual journey. Wherever my journey takes me, I know it will continue to make a great story. With the heart of a fire dragon, my life will always be full of adventures.

ACKNOWLEDGMENTS

When I started writing this book I was in my twenties. It was therapy for me as I learned how to weave my way through intimate relationships. When I met my husband, I put the project aside and didn't look at it for over a decade.

I started to get the itch to write again a couple of years ago. My story from years ago popped into my head. However, after years of burning through many computers, my files were gone. Months later, after many failed attempts at starting a new story, I found my manuscript when cleaning out paper files at home. I only had a few pages to start with, but that was enough. I rediscovered my writing groove.

When I finished my first draft, I felt uneasy with the combination of relationships and mystical experiences that I'd sewn together. After polling my yoga students, who said it was part of my journey and should be combined, I presented it to my author friend, Stella, asking her to make a first pass on editing. When she was done, I sat on the hard wood floor of her living room with her infant son. She asked me about my childhood, which was missing from my pages. She said she wanted to know how I became the person in my story.

After a few weeks of hemming and hawing over whether I really needed to go there (after all, it was hard enough to live through it the first time around), I finally understood. I spent the next three months writing my manuscript all over again.

Without the courage of my yoga students, and the advice of Stella, I would never have completed the story I was meant to tell. Thank you to Lawrence and Tammi at Sunbury Press for taking a chance on this first time author, and to Lawrence's grandmother who influenced his decision from the "other side." Thank you to my editor, Amanda, whose email back to me after reading through the manuscript several times, brought tears to my eyes as she said that I could actually tell a story and weave those pieces together well.

Thank you to my girlfriends for reading through my first draft, your advice and support. A huge thank you to my soul sister Arabella, who is not only my best friend, but comrade-in-arms in this life—God love her, she took the brunt of dealing with me over the last seventeen years, listening to me prattle on and on about life, love, and writing. I cannot forget my mother and her family for their influence on my life.

To my husband and my daughter, thank you for your understanding on those many days and nights when I would sit in my "office" (AKA our back porch) ignoring the world and writing. You both are the joy of my life. I cannot believe I am so blessed, so lucky, to walk this life with you. Thank you for your unconditional, unending love.

This book was originally written as a diary of sorts. It morphed from a story for single ladies, to a piece of me to give to my daughter, to a story for my yoga students. Now, it is for you, dear reader. I hope you find something to take with you along on your own journey.

39202858R00108

Made in the USA
Lexington, KY
11 February 2015